Armageddon!

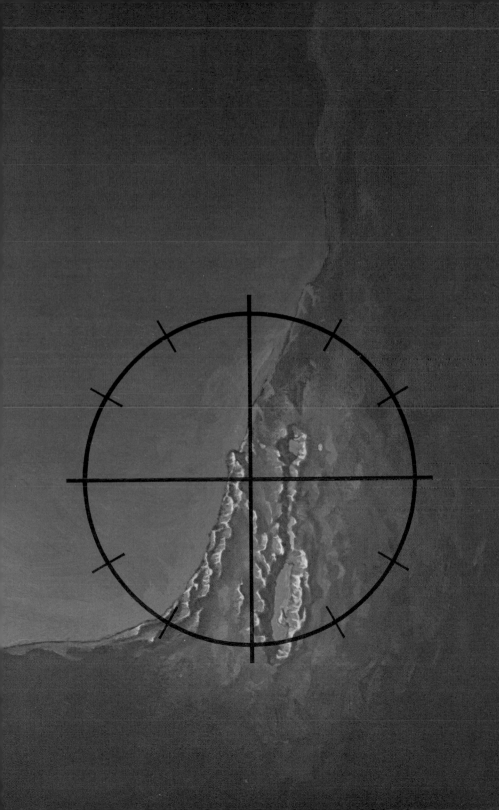

Armageddon!

by
Edgar C. James

MOODY PRESS
CHICAGO

All Scripture quotations, except those noted otherwise, are from the *New American Standard Bible,* © 1960, 1962, 1963, 1968, 1971, 1972, 1973, 1975, and 1977 by The Lockman Foundation, and are used by permission.

Chapters 6, 7, 8, 9, and 10 appeared in slightly different form in the October, November, December 1980, and the January and February 1981 issues of *Moody Monthly* magazine.

Library of Congress Cataloging in Publication Data

James, Edgar C.
  Armageddon!

  1. Bible—Prophecies.   2. Eschatology.   3. Future
life.   I. Title.
BS647.2.J35   236'.9   81-9558
ISBN 0-8024-0297-6   AACR2

Second Printing, 1981

Printed in the United States of America

Contents

1
Dreams, Visions, and the Word of God

With all the problems we face today, how can we know the future?

"It was a frustrating experience," a woman confided. "I thought my life was really on track. But now with three children and a broken marriage, how can I be sure of what will happen next?"

"I don't know where to turn," a businessman told me. "World problems really affect our business. How can I know for sure what will happen next year or even next week?"

8 • Armageddon!

"Maybe I shouldn't worry, but I do," a neighbor confessed. "I work at my job and try to keep my life in order. But these news reports are scary. Nations keep moving against each other with threats and wars. Where can I turn to find out where this world is headed?"

We live with problems on every hand; the problems of the family, the problems of the economy, the problems of the nations. All of us are searching for answers. Where is this world headed, and how can we make sense out of our own lives? All the standards of previous years are being overturned. How can we plan our lives when there is no anchor?

"This thing in the Middle East really troubles me," said a friend. "I have two sons, and now with draft registration I don't know what is going to happen. The superpowers are jockeying for position, volcanoes are erupting, the plug on energy could be pulled, and my life-style is falling apart. Armageddon is surely around the corner. Can anybody know the future?"

Some are seeking answers from fortune tellers. "I couldn't believe I was going to such a person," a politician told me. "But I needed help, and I thought that was the way. The advice I received, though, was dead wrong!"

Others are seeking answers from psychics. "Predictions for Next Year—Ten Prominent Psychics Tell All," the headline reads. But a careful tabulation of such predictions finds that most never come true.

Still others are seeking answers in astrology, the view that the sun, moon, and stars can influence human affairs.

"Our home was a very expensive one," a woman told me. "It was secluded in a lovely wooded area. But when I saw my chart and the way the planet Mars, standing for fires and accidents, and Saturn, standing for restriction and loss, were in exact conjunction with one another, I reached for the phone.

" 'I want to increase my insurance,' I told my broker. The fire never came, but at least I was protected!"

Astrology today is enjoying its greatest boom in history. First used by the Sumerians, it held an important place in Babylonia, Egypt, and Rome. Today there are whole columns on the subject in most major newspapers. Many books and magazines about it are printed each year.

Businessmen invest in the stock market according to their signs. Politicians use astrology to guide them in important decisions. Entertainment people use it to decide which roles they will play. When meeting people in some areas it is not uncommon to hear the greeting "What sign are you?"

Yet a careful examination of the subject shows that much subjective interpretation is used. In addition, predictions are so general they are not valid, or they are completely wrong. A small percentage may come true, but seldom exactly as predicted or within the specified time frame.

There are many others who use their own dreams and visions to guide them.

"I've had a good life," said one woman, "but I haven't been happy. My husband is a good man, a leading surgeon in this city. But when we were going together, we had many arguments and were about to break up several times.

"During a rather stormy session, I had a dream," she continued. "In my dream I saw an angel at the foot of my bed who said, 'Go ahead and marry him, and I will bless the marriage.' I went ahead, but life has been anything but peaceful. I wonder if dreams really can be trusted."

Although dreams may reflect our own thinking and therefore relieve psychological pressure, they are unreliable guides to the future. They only mirror our own images. They do not provide clear answers.

How can any humanly contrived system, whether fortune tellers, psychics, astrologers, or dreams, give accurate guidance for the future? How can they do anything but extend the historical patterns of man? They cannot predict change. They cannot predict outside forces. And if they cannot do that on an individual level, how can they do it on the national and world levels?

There is a book that gives assurance for the future. Within its pages it tells of the future of the nations. From its words we learn what will happen to this world. And with its instruction, we see how to run our lives.

What is its name? It is the Bible.

Centuries ago prophets told of events that would happen not only in their day but many years in the future. Some of them told of the whole span of world history. Others told of One who would come to relieve men of their oppression. Still others spoke of upheavals in the crust of the earth, events that would occur in the Middle East, and a righteous kingdom that would come upon this earth.

Some people in that day thought their dreams and visions were more authoritative than those prophetic words. Other people thought their own experiences would command their lives. To combat that wrong thinking, one writer of Scripture told of one of the greatest experiences he or anyone could possibly have had. He once was an eyewitness to Jesus Christ, not just as He lived among men on this earth, but when He appeared in great glory before three of His disciples. "We were eyewitnesses of His majesty," Peter says (2 Peter 1:16).

But the apostle goes on. He points out that even though that was a great experience for him, we have a more certain word of prophecy (2 Peter 1:19). We have the Scriptures, which are accurate records from God that carefully convey what will happen in the future.

With all the problems we face on every hand, we

need someplace to which we can turn. In such a world as ours, there must be someplace where there is hope. With such uncertain times as these, can we not have an anchor that will give steadfastness and stability to our lives?

The Bible speaks of a time of great trouble that will come and encompass the whole earth. It also tells about the nations of the world and what will happen to them. It speaks of Russia and her allies, a great western confederacy, kings of the east, and more. It tells how those people will come together in earth's final war, the campaign of Armageddon. In addition, it tells of the hope for this world, the reign of Christ upon this earth. It even describes what will happen when we die and where we will spend eternity. In light of all we face today, the Bible alone provides clear answers.

Many people today are going to spiritists, astrologers, and psychics. They are determining their signs and plotting their charts. They are traveling miles to hear some modern prophetess speak on politics or the stock market. Would it not be better to walk across the living room and pick up the Bible to see what it accurately predicts?

Why should we be so interested in Bible prophecy? Why is it important? Certainly it is not just because we are curious. All of us would like to know about the future. But knowledge in and of itself makes people proud. If it does not affect life, it gives a false sense of security.

One reason Bible prophecy is so important is

that it *confirms the authority of the Word of God.* Although the Bible claims to be from God and shows remarkable unity between its human authors, how can we be sure it is from God? The fulfillment of Bible prophecy confirms that great fact.

Much of the Scripture, nearly a third, was prophetic at the time it was written. Although there is a great deal yet to be fulfilled, many events already have taken place. As we examine those and find how minute and accurate the prophecies were and how completely they were fulfilled, we can conclude the entire Scripture must be from God. And certainly if the Bible speaks authoritatively in the area of prophecy, does it not speak authoritatively in every other area of life?

Another reason Bible prophecy is so important is that it *shows the power of God.* There are many examples of God's power in the past. Those include Creation, the crossing of the Red Sea by the children of Israel, and the capstone, the resurrection of Jesus Christ. As important as those events were in the past, you and I are faced with the wrongs of this world. We are witnessing nations moving against each other. We are products of family and home problems. We are seeing people being torn apart.

Is there anything that can right the wrongs of this world? Is there anything that can solve our problems?

It is at this very point that prophecy gives guidance. It shows that God's power is not limited. It gives hope that the Lord can do what He has promised.

One day Christ will come to this earth and set up His kingdom here. One day there will be a time of righteousness among the nations. And one day God will create a new heaven and new earth and a place for all of us to dwell.

The day of God's power is not over. He is able to do all He has promised. There is hope in Him. And if that is true for the future, is He not moving the events of this world to His desired goals? And does He not have the power to enable us to live for Him today?

Bible prophecy is also important because it *shows us the purposes of God.* By what God has told us in His Book, we know what He is planning to do. He has removed the cloud over where things are moving today. We can know what is going to happen, and we can know where we fit in.

What kind of lives would we be able to live if all we had were newspapers, newsmagazines, and television reports? We would live very frustrated lives. We would be reacting to each and every event in our world and thinking of it as coincidental and haphazard. We would not see any plan. We would wonder if life were worth living at all.

But God has given us much more than that. He has drawn back the veil to show us His purposes. He has told us where this world is headed. We can know why He is doing things. Without God's knowledge of the future we would be like ships without rudders. We would not know where we were going or how to get there.

Bible prophecy also *gives peace to those who know the Lord.* Jesus said, "Let not your heart be troubled" (John 14:1). We can have confidence in Him because He is in control.

As a child can be at peace in his father's arms even though both are in a storm-tossed boat at sea, we can be at peace in this world if we are in our Father's arms. It is not our circumstance that gives peace. Rather, it is where we have placed our security. When we are in the center of God's will, we can rest in Him in the midst of the storms of life. We can have peace in our world as we have confidence in our God.

Perhaps the most important reason for knowing Bible prophecy is that it *gives purity of life.* As we learn what will happen in the future, it should have an effect on our daily living. We will want to demonstrate the life of Christ in the world in which we live.

Throughout the New Testament, the promise of the return of Christ is always coupled with how we are to live in light of such a promise. For instance, Peter writes, "Therefore, beloved, since you look for these things, be diligent to be found by Him in peace, spotless and blameless" (2 Peter 3:14). John admonishes that "everyone who has this hope fixed on Him purifies himself, just as He is pure" (1 John 3:3). The hope of Christ's return should make our present living more holy.

Many are looking to their own experiences or human guides to find out about the future. But since it is God who controls the future, should we not look to Him? When we do, we will have peace and confidence in Him for now as well as then. Such contentment will also help us demonstrate His life and teaching in our present world.

So to find out what is going to happen, read on.

2
Look What Has Happened

The applicant brought all the forms as he entered the office for the interview.

"How long did you work at this position?" asked the personnel officer as he pointed with his pencil to a line on one of the forms.

"Six years."

"And what did you do when you worked here?" questioned the officer as he pointed to another line.

"I was foreman."

After checking several more lines and asking the appropriate questions, the officer concluded the interview by saying, "I'll have to check these references and get back to you. I'll just call you at your home phone number."

Days passed, but Bob heard nothing. He knew he had done a good job at all the places he had worked. But he also knew it was company policy to make a thorough check. Finally the phone rang, and he was invited to come for another interview.

"We have checked out all your references," said the personnel officer, "and we believe you can do the job here. You are hired, Bob, and you will begin the first of next month. We believe that what you have done in the past proves what you can do here. We are proud to have you."

Just as when seeking employment what one will do in the future is proved by what one has done in the past, so it is with Bible prophecy.

Nearly one-third of the Bible was prophetic at the time it was given. But much of that has already been fulfilled. There are prophecies of cities, kingdoms, and people that were carefully given by prophets of old and have been accurately fulfilled. If we are to see how the other prophecies will come to pass, it is important to see some of those that already have been fulfilled.

One exciting Bible prophecy that was minutely fulfilled was one that concerned the city of Tyre. This city was located on the shores of the Mediterranean Sea, just north of Israel in modern-day Lebanon. It was between the cities of Acre and Sidon in old Phoenicia.

Tyre was known in Solomon's day as one of the great cities of the world. It enjoyed special prosperity under King Hiram (980–947 B.C.). He was the one who provided much of the manpower and material for the construction of the Temple as well as for David's and Solomon's palaces (2 Samuel 5:11–12; 2 Chronicles 2).

But the leaders of that city, although helping Israel in many ways, did not recognize the God of Israel. In fact, they turned their backs on Him. They wanted to make money from Him but did not want to worship Him.

What would happen? God told the people that He would utterly destroy the city.

The decision to destroy Tyre was not arbitrary. That city, in boasting of her sin, was a bad example to other nations, especially the nation Israel. It was because of her sin and pride that God promised He would wipe her from the face of the earth.

How would God do that? One way was to bring many nations against the coastal fortress. They would come against her as "the sea brings up its waves" (Ezekiel 26:3). They would break her down and destroy her towers. They would also scrape the debris from her and "make her a bare rock" (Ezekiel 26:4).

What else would God do? He would make the destruction so great that never again would any city be built on the same spot. The city's site would be a "place for the spreading of nets" (Ezekiel 26:5), as a reminder of God's destructive power.

The daughters of Tyre would be slain by the sword so the world would know a sovereign God, a God of holiness and justice, was at work during that time.

As one carefully examines the prophecy of that destruction, one can see it is unlike any manmade prophecy of our day. Rather, it is specific, it is detailed, and it shows that somehow God would have to move many events if He were literally to fulfill His Word.

How was the prophecy fulfilled? In one of the most remarkable sagas of history, God moved the kings of the earth to accomplish His purpose.

One person the Lord used was Nebuchadnezzar, king of Babylon. God even predicted what would happen. He said, "Behold, I will bring upon Tyre from the north Nebuchadnezzar king of Babylon" (Ezekiel 26:7).

Nebuchadnezzar was to come down, seize the city, and cast a mount around her. He would break down her towers, use battering rams against her, and utterly destroy the city that had so boasted against the Lord.

What else would happen? The hoofs of the horses would trample the streets (Ezekiel 26:11). The people would be slain. The strong pillars of the buildings would come to the ground. The houses would be destroyed. Timbers and debris would be all over the place.

As if a special hand was upon Nebuchadnezzar, he and his armies minutely and accurately fulfilled every verse of this passage. He besieged the city for thirteen years and completely destroyed it. He left the rubble where it fell, trampled by his horses' hooves. He slew the people and brought the houses to the ground. He did exactly as God had predicted.

But the city of Tyre was built in two parts. One section of the city was built on the mainland, and that was the city Nebuchadnezzar destroyed in 585–572 B.C. in fulfillment of Ezekiel's prophecy. But the other section of the city remained. It was built on an island in the Mediterranean Sea, a few miles from the mainland.

When Nebuchadnezzar came against the mainland city of Tyre, many of the people were killed, but some escaped to the island city of Tyre. There they continued to defy the Lord. Their protection was the sea that surrounded the island. No one could penetrate their defenses. Nebuchadnezzar could do what he wanted with the mainland city, but how could anyone destroy a city so cleverly protected by water?

The prophecy God gave Ezekiel spoke about more than trampling the rubble of the city with the hooves of horses. God said, "And I will make you a bare rock; you will be a place for the spreading of nets. You will be built no more" (Ezekiel 26:14). Nebuchadnezzar had not made the city as bare as a rock, nor had he destroyed the island city. How would God fulfill that part of the prophecy?

God did fulfill this prophecy through another

man, Alexander the Great. In 332 B.C., almost two hundred years after Nebuchadnezzar, the Greek general Alexander came down and besieged the city of Tyre, which by that time had rebuilt itself. But Alexander did something else. He besieged the island city for six months. Finally, after destroying the mainland city, he saw he could not capture the island city.

But did that stop him? Not at all. When Alexander saw he could not capture the island city, he went back to the mainland city. He took all the rubble left by Nebuchadnezzar and pushed it into the sea. By doing so, he was able to make a great causeway out to the island, over which he drove his armies, and was able to completely destroy the island city of Tyre.

It is possible to visit the city of Tyre today. But modern Tyre is built on an entirely different site than was the original city. What happened to that original site? It is now used by fishermen as the place "for the spreading of nets" (Ezekiel 26:14). Although written in detail hundreds of years before it happened, this remarkable passage is today completely, specifically fulfilled.

There are other illustrations of fulfilled Bible prophecy. Probably the greatest one is that of the first coming of Jesus Christ. Throughout the Old Testament, prophets told how Christ would come to this earth, live, suffer and die, and be raised again. Although we may think of prophecy as relating to only the second coming of Christ, much of it concerns His first coming and has been completely fulfilled.

For instance, the place of Christ's birth was predicted. Seven hundred fifty years before He was ever born, the Old Testament predicted that His birthplace would be Bethlehem (Micah 5:2). Why Bethlehem? If a promotion specialist of today were to pick the place for the King of kings to be born, would he not have picked Rome, Athens, or at least Jerusalem? But Bethlehem, which means "house of bread," was the city of David and David's line. God predicted it would be Bethlehem.

How was the world moved so that Christ would be born in Bethlehem? Mary and Joseph lived in Nazareth, seventy miles to the north. Although seventy miles in our day may not be much, in that day it was a great distance, especially for a woman who was about to give birth.

The Lord moved in a Roman emperor's heart so that a census was required, not at the place where people grew up, which was the ordinary way, but at the place of their lineage. Since both Mary and Joseph were related to King David, they went to the city of Bethlehem. In that way the remarkable prophecy of Micah, written seven and a half centuries before, was completely fulfilled.

Why was Jesus to come to this earth? The Old Testament foretold that as well. The prophet wrote that He would "bring good news to the afflicted; He has sent me to bind up the brokenhearted, to proclaim liberty to captives, and freedom to prisoners; to proclaim the favorable year of the LORD" (Isaiah 61:1-2). That was the emphasis of Jesus' ministry. He worked miracles and dealt with the afflicted and brokenhearted. His message was one of good news and liberty. He came to seek and to save that which was lost (Luke 19:10). Later, Jesus would read from that Old Testament passage, and say, "Today this Scripture has been fulfilled in your hearing" (Luke 4:21).

One of the major Old Testament prophecies of Christ concerned His death. That was spoken of by many prophets, from Moses (Genesis 3:15) to Malachi. Perhaps the greatest passages are Psalm 22 and Isaiah 53.

Psalm 22 emphasizes the history of Christ's death—records the events that were actually to take place. Isaiah 53 points to the meaning of that death, the explanation. He died for the sins of the world.

There are many statements in Psalm 22 that were actually spoken at the time of Christ's death. For instance, on the cross Jesus said, "My God, my God, why hast Thou forsaken me?" (Psalm 22:1; cf. Matthew 27:46). The psalmist predicts they would pierce "my hands and my feet" (Psalm 22:16). It shows His bones would not be broken (Psalm 22:17; John 19:31-34). The soldiers would "divide my garments among them, and for my clothing they cast lots" (Psalm 22:18; Matthew 27:35). The crucifixion of Christ was carried out by those who had no knowledge of those predictions. Somehow and in some way, they did exactly as the psalmist predicted. Is it not true that only God could order such events?

Isaiah 53 gives the meaning of that death. It was the Lord who "caused the iniquity of us all to fall on Him" (Isaiah 53:6). Jesus Christ became the sin-bearer of mankind. All who accept that provision as their own receive the salvation that He alone can offer. The death of Christ was no accident, but was specifically predicted in the Old Testament and was completely fulfilled.

The resurrection of Christ was also predicted. Not only would Jesus die, said the prophets, but He would also be raised again from the dead. Notice the passage, "Neither wilt Thou allow Thy Holy One to undergo decay" (Psalm 16:10). What does that mean? It is that when Jesus died, His body would not have time to decay because it would be raised from the dead. That was the point Peter made on the day of Pentecost when he quoted from this Old Testament passage (Acts 2:27). Peter declared that the same Jesus who was crucified was also the one who was raised. The Old Testament prophecies of Christ's first coming have been completely fulfilled.

What lessons can we learn from fulfilled Bible

prophecy? One lesson is that it shows the authority of the Word of God. This Bible is a book that man could not write if he would. It is the inspired Word of God. Fulfilled Bible prophecies confirm that fact.

Fulfilled Bible prophecy also shows how other Bible prophecies will be fulfilled. If God has fulfilled the first coming of Christ in a literal way, will not the second coming of Christ be fulfilled in the same way? We can rely on the truth of God's Word. Prophecies of the future will be fulfilled accurately.

If we can trust God to fulfill the prophecies of Scripture, we can also trust the promises He gives us. We know that His Word works because we have seen the way it worked in the past. Is He not the kind of God we need to serve? Is He not the kind of God we need to trust?

But what about unfulfilled Bible prophecy? We turn to consider that next.

3
The Great
Snatch

The day was bright and cheery, and the road in front of the colonial-style house appeared empty. Sally had finished her afternoon nap and was ready to go out to play.

"I'll just be out front, Mother," she called. "I have my wagon and scooter. I'll play till Daddy comes home."

Sally busied herself with her toys, but soon ran out of space in the front yard. She thought she would try the street, but would keep close to the curb. An occasional car did come by, but the drivers easily saw her and went around her.

As time went on, however, Sally edged toward the middle of the street. All of a sudden—it seemed as if from nowhere—a delivery truck came barreling down the street, aimed right at Sally. It looked as if there was no hope.

Coming home early that night, however, was Sally's father. His quick eyes took in the total scene. When he saw the truck, he knew there was only one thing to do. He dropped everything, his paper and briefcase, and made a mad dash for Sally. Swooping her in his arms, he ran to the other side of the street, just as the truck passed them both.

"That was a close one, Daddy," Sally said as they both tried to catch their breath. A wise father, out of love for his child, had quickly snatched her out of the path of certain disaster.

One day the Lord is going to come and snatch away all believers to be with Him. Jesus said, "I will come again, and receive you to Myself; that where I am, there you may be also" (John 14:3).

Sometimes that event is called the "rapture" of the church. The word *rapture* is the Latin translation of the phrase "caught up" used by Scripture to describe that event (1 Thessalonians 4:17). One day Jesus will come to catch up the church from earth to heaven.

What will happen in the rapture? Jesus first discussed this subject when He was alone with His disciples. They were together in the upper room right before His death, and Jesus was relating to His disciples some of the things that would take place in the future. He made some important announcements to them.

One announcement He made concerned His betrayal. He said, "One of you will betray Me" (John 13:21). The disciples were mystified, for they had been His close companions for over three years. They asked who would betray Him. Jesus said it would be the one to whom He gave the sop, a small morsel of bread. He gave it to Judas, and when He did, Judas left the room.

What did that mean? It meant Judas was going to commence his act of betrayal. It also meant that what Jesus was about to tell the disciples was only for those who truly believed in Him. He was going to share with them truths about the Holy Spirit in their lives, truths about prayer, and truths about His coming for them.

Another announcement Jesus made concerned His death. He said, "Now is the Son of Man glorified" (John 13:31)—a most significant statement. Throughout the gospel of John, Jesus told many people that His hour had not yet come. He was saying that the purpose for which He had come into the world had not yet arrived. But now it had. He would now be glorified. First had come the ministry and teaching that led up to the cross—now the time had come for Him to be delivered up for the sins of the world.

Another announcement Jesus made concerned His separation from them. He would soon be leaving them. "I am with you a little while longer.... 'Where I am going, you cannot come'" (John 13:33). The one who came to be king of the world would now be leaving that world.

Peter could not understand Jesus' statement. Had the disciples not been with Him for those years? Should they not be in the forefront of the kingdom when it was established? How could the king, of all people, say He was leaving just when He was needed most?

Jesus explained that although He would soon be leaving, believers would follow Him later. He had work to do now, but they would be able to come later. He spoke, of course, of His ascension.

What was Christ's program? What was His purpose in leaving? Jesus called upon the disciples to have faith in the person of God as well as Himself. "Let not your heart be troubled; believe in God, believe also in Me" (John 14:1). The Lord knows what He is doing, what He is going to accomplish. Our confidence must be placed in Him. What He demands is obedience.

Jesus was leaving to prepare a place for those who trust Him. He said, "In My Father's house are many dwelling places ... I go to prepare a place for you" (John 14:2).

Jesus was probably picturing a large Roman house. Such homes were built in large squares, with an open section in the middle. The open section would have a garden watered by the rain, which could also be caught for cooking and drinking. Around the open section would be many rooms. Some of those rooms would be used for eating, others for cooking, and still others for bedrooms.

When one of the sons of the family would get married, he would bring his bride back to the home and live in a suite of rooms. It was that arrangement Jesus described to His disciples. He said that in His Father's house are many rooms, or dwelling places. There is enough space for all. One day the Bridegroom is going to come and take the bride back to the Father's house.

What promise is there that the Bridegroom is going to come for the bride? Jesus said, "I will come again, and receive you to Myself" (John 14:3). Although one may send servants to do many things, one does not send a servant to get married. Jesus will not send an angel or servant for His bride, but will one day come Himself.

What, then, was Jesus' purpose in leaving? It was to "prepare" or "refurbish" the dwelling places. Jesus is not just constructing, but exquisitely decorating that place. It is later described in the book of Revelation as the New Jerusalem (Revelation 21:8—22:9), a city with walls and gates. It is foursquare, with a river of life flowing through it. Can you imagine how beautiful that city will be if our Lord is preparing it for us?

Heaven is not only a place, however; it is also a

Person. Jesus said, "No one comes to the Father, but through Me" (John 14:6). Heaven is where God is, and one day we will be caught up to be there with Him. That is the promise of the rapture.

The word "dwelling place" (John 14:2) is also used in the next chapter in the "abiding" life (John 15:4). In the first passage the noun form of the word is used, and in the second passage the verb form of the same word is used. That helps us understand that one day we will be taken to our *abiding* place. But now you and I can have the abiding life, the same kind of life we will have then. We can now enjoy the heavenly life by having fellowship with our Lord. God is not only preparing a place for His bride, but He is also preparing His bride for her place.

What will happen to the believer when Christ comes for him? Those who have died, of course, will be resurrected. But all believers who are alive when Christ comes for His church will be changed. The apostle promises that "we shall not all sleep, but we shall all be changed" (1 Corinthians 15:51).

In the Old Testament there were two people that were directly taken to heaven without seeing death. One of those was Enoch, and the other was Elijah. But God promises that one day when Christ comes for His church an entire generation of believers will not see death, will not "sleep," but will be changed. Their natural physical bodies will be changed into those new bodies that God promises for us. They will at that time be like Christ (1 John 3:2).

How fast will that change take place? It will be instantaneous. It will be "in the twinkling of an eye" (1 Corinthians 15:52). It is a miracle by God that will happen when He comes for us.

When will it take place? It will be at the "last trumpet" (1 Corinthians 15:52). Although trumpets were sometimes used during Old Testament times for judgment, they were also used for worship and celebration. They were used for judgment when the walls of the city of Jericho fell down. For worship and celebration, they were blown to gather the people to the feasts of Israel. Trumpets will be used for judgment in end times, as is foretold in the book of Revelation (Revelation 8-11). But they will also be used in celebration, as seen in 1 Corinthians 15. This is a time of victory, a time of joy and celebration. The Lord is victorious over death and is coming for His church.

The people in the church at Thessalonica were having trouble understanding what would happen in the rapture. They were afraid that those already dead would miss out on the catching away of the church. The Lord, through the apostle Paul, pointed out that those who had already died in the Lord would also be sharing in that great event.

The information the apostle provides in this section is for believers ("brethren," 1 Thessalonians 4:13). The prospect for them is different than for those who have "no hope."

Upon what is the resurrection of the believer based? It is dependent on the resurrection of Christ. He is the firstfruits of resurrection (1 Corinthians 15:23), the first one to be raised, who will never die again. Since Jesus has been raised from the dead, those who have died in Him will also be raised (1 Thessalonians 4:14).

The promise the apostle gives is so important that it comes by direct authority of the Lord Himself (1 Thessalonians 4:15). Those who are alive and remain will not precede those who already have died in the rapture. Both groups will be united to Christ at the same time.

What will happen? First will be Christ's return (1 Thessalonians 4:16). The Lord Himself will descend from heaven. He is Himself coming for His church. To announce that event will be a shout, a voice, and a trumpet. The shout will be a military command, and all who are in Christ will hear it. The voice is that of the chief angel, the leader of the angelic beings. The trumpet is the trumpet of God, a trumpet blown for rejoicing and celebration.

What else will happen? The dead "in Christ" will rise first. All those who have trusted Christ as Savior in this age will be resurrected. In addition, those who are then alive, that entire generation of believers, will also be changed. Then both groups, the dead and alive, will be caught up to be with the Lord (1 Thessalonians 4:17). They will be snatched away, or raptured, from the earth.

What effect will that event have upon those who remain on the earth? Certainly some will think of the testimony of believers. But most of those who remain will be so busy in their own affairs that they will have little time for the things of God. That is why the Lord will send vast judgments upon the earth.

But you and I should always be living in light of the rapture. We do not know when it will take place. As we look at the events happening in our world today, we believe it may be very soon. But we should always be ready. The apostle believed he would be part of those then alive ("we who are alive"), and every generation has had that same hope. But whether the Lord takes us by death or the rapture, we must be faithful to Him, using every opportunity of service for Him.

One day He will come for us. There will be a great reunion with the Lord. We will meet Him "in the air" (1 Thessalonians 4:17). Although we live for Him and serve Him, we have not as yet visibly seen Him. But one day we will meet Him face to face.

These are words of comfort and reassurance (1 Thessalonians 4:18). These are words of tenderness and affection, of promise and hope. Although we face many problems today, we look forward to the time our Lord will come for us. But until then, we should be faithful and obedient, living pure lives before Him. We must do all He has commanded as we wait for His return.

4
More Trouble Is Coming

It was surrounded by lush green forests and rolling rivers, rich farmland and prime vacationland. Sixty miles north of Vancouver, Washington, it was the fifth tallest mountain in the state.

On a quiet Sunday in May, Mount St. Helens erupted with a force 2,500 times that of the atomic bomb dropped on Hiroshima. In one gigantic blast, 1,500 feet blew off the top. All of a sudden the huge mountain became the thirtieth tallest in the state.

Everywhere one looked there were seas of black and gray volcanic rock. The ash from the disaster

blew over everything. The farmland and vacationland quickly turned to wasteland. The surrounding rivers, forests, and woodlands became desolate.

Volcanoes, earthquakes, and floods are occur-
ring more frequently in our day. Fires, storms,
and pestilence are everywhere around us. Many
are wondering if they will make it into next month
or next year. The disasters of our day are causing
people to ask, "Is this the end of the world?"

The Bible predicts there is coming a time when
great devastation will reign upon the earth. There
will be great affliction and persecution. There will
be earthquakes, wars, famine, pestilence, and lawlessness.

Jesus called it the time of "great tribulation."
He said, "there will be great tribulation, such as
has not occurred since the beginning of the world
until now, nor ever shall" (Matthew 24:21).

Throughout the course of history there have
been earthquakes, famines, floods, and fires.
People have died in plagues. But Jesus taught that
one day unprecedented trouble is coming upon
this earth. It will be completely different from
anything that has occurred or will occur.

Jesus had told the disciples they could expect
some kind of trouble and tribulation in this world
(John 16:33). Because the world hated Christ, it
would hate those who followed Him. Those who
came after the disciples and followed the Lord
would also face such hardships. They would en-

dure the problems and pressures of being servants for God in an ungodly place.

But in Matthew 24–25 Jesus was talking about an *unprecedented* time of trouble that will come upon the earth. Although we may suffer for the Lord today, we are not yet in the time period called "the tribulation." The events of our day are foreshadowing what is yet to take place. More trouble is coming.

The physical and spiritual phenomena during that time will be so unendurable that God Himself will have to stop them. Jesus said, "And unless those days had been cut short, no life would have been saved" (Matthew 24:22). In other words, if God did not cut short, or interrupt, this period of time, the entire world would perish. Jesus, however, is going to interrupt it. He is going to bring it to a close by returning to the earth to set up His kingdom. It is because of the people who will be saved at that time that Jesus will cut short those days.

The Tribulation was described by the Old Testament prophets. They called it "a time of distress" (Daniel 12:1), "the time of Jacob's distress" (Jeremiah 30:7), and a "day of trouble and distress" (Zephaniah 1:15). Jesus, right before His death, reminded His disciples of that period.

The disciples showed Jesus the buildings of the Temple. The Temple had been begun by Herod the Great in 20 B.C., but it would not be finished until A.D. 64. It was a beautiful place.

As Jesus was looking at the Temple, He made an unusual statement. He said, "Truly I say to you, not one stone here shall be left upon another, which will not be torn down" (Matthew 24:2).

The disciples were dumbfounded. They could not understand how a building so huge and beautiful, so many years in construction, would suddenly be destroyed. So they came to Jesus privately, when He was on the Mount of Olives, and asked Him what He meant.

The disciples asked three questions. First, they asked, "Tell us, when will these things be?" (Matthew 24:3). They wanted to know when the Temple would be destroyed. The answer Jesus gave to that question is recorded in Luke 21:20–24. It would be "when you see Jerusalem surrounded by armies" (Luke 21:20).

In A.D. 70, Titus and his Roman armies surrounded the city of Jerusalem for six months while they waited for orders from Rome to attack. Some Christians, in response to those words from Christ, took the opportunity to flee from the city. The people who remained were destroyed by the Roman armies when they came through and leveled the city completely. Not one stone stood upon the other. The words of Jesus were true.

The second question the disciples asked was, "What will be the sign of Your coming?" (Matthew 24:3). Jesus answered that question in Matthew 24:29–31.

One day many things will happen in the sky.

The sun will be darkened, the moon will not give light, and stars will fall (Matthew 24:29). Then the sign of the Son of Man will appear (Matthew 24:30). That may be the lightning described or perhaps the glory of Christ as He returns. It is at that point that Jesus will come to the earth to set up His kingdom. He will come "with power and great glory" (Matthew 24:30). His coming to set up His kingdom will be after the Tribulation, whereas His coming for the church (the rapture) will precede that time.

The third question the disciples asked was what would be the signs "of the end of the age" (Matthew 24:3). Jesus answered that question first, as recorded in Matthew 24:4–28.

The "end of the age" is that period of time right before the return of Christ to this earth to set up His kingdom. It is the time of Tribulation, the time when great judgment will be poured out upon the earth. After those events, Jesus will return to put down all enemies under His feet and to rule the nations with a rod of iron. Many of the events of today may foreshadow events of the Tribulation. The event that begins the time period is the signing of a special covenant between the Antichrist and the nation Israel (Daniel 9:27).

Jesus enumerates several events that will take place during the Tribulation. He says, "For many will come in My name, saying, 'I am the Christ,' and will mislead many" (Matthew 24:5). Although there have been many throughout the years who claimed to be messiahs, the Antichrist will during the Tribulation mislead many more by counterfeiting the miracles of God and usurping the worship of God.

There will also be wars and rumors of wars. The great military campaign of the Antichrist will culminate in Armageddon, the final battle on earth. Although many wars have occurred throughout history, that will be a time of unprecedented bloodshed.

What else will happen? There will also be famines and earthquakes (Matthew 24:7). Those are further described in the book of Revelation. Whole cities will crumble (Revelation 6:12; 16:18–19). Could the famines and earthquakes of today be foreshadowing such events?

But all of those are just the beginning of that time period (Matthew 24:8). The last half of the period, known as the "great tribulation" (Matthew 24:21), will have even more intense events.

There will be anti-Semitism (Matthew 24:9), many will be falling away from the truth, and hatred will increase (Matthew 24:10). There will be false prophets (Matthew 24:11). There will be increased lawlessness, as people turn their backs on all moral law (Matthew 24:12).

The Antichrist, the one spoken of by Daniel the prophet, will stand in "the holy place" (Matthew 24:15). That, of course, refers to the Temple in Israel. One day it will be rebuilt, either during the beginning of the Tribulation or perhaps even sooner. The Antichrist will put himself in the Temple and call himself God. He will even seek to be worshiped as God (2 Thessalonians 2:3-4).

Much of the book of Revelation describes the same period of time. The apostle John records that there will be three series of judgments poured out upon the earth. Those are the seal judgments (Revelation 6), the trumpet judgments (Revelation 8-9), and the bowl, or vial, judgments (Revelation 15-16).

The seal judgments are judgments written in a book, or scroll. There are seven seals on that scroll, and as each seal is broken, a judgment is read. The seal judgments concern a false messiah who will come, worldwide warfare, inflation and famine, death, martyrdom, and many natural disasters in the sun, moon, stars, and earth.

When the seventh seal is broken (Revelation 8:1), the trumpet judgments are blown, for the seventh seal contains the trumpet judgments. There is a telescopic effect. In a similar way, when the seventh trumpet is blown, the bowl, or vial, judgments are poured out, for the seventh trumpet contains the bowl judgments.

What are the trumpet judgments? The first is a judgment on the vegetation systems of the earth. Next the transportation systems are affected. Then the sanitation systems of the earth are judged. Next, heavenly bodies, the sun, moon, and stars, are affected. The fifth is a judgment of pestilence. A horde of locusts will torment the peoples of the earth. Finally, the sixth trumpet is a judgment of death.

The bowl, or vial, judgments are the last series of judgments to be poured out during that time (Revelation 15–16). Today, when we say that our cup is full, we mean our cup of blessing is full. One day, however, God's cup, or bowl, of judgment will be full and will be poured out upon the earth.

What are the bowl judgments? The first is malignant sores that come upon those who have the mark of the Beast (Antichrist). The next one smites the seas. The third affects the rivers of the earth. The following bowl judgment scorches people with great heat. The fifth sends darkness upon the earth. The sixth is when the Euphrates River is dried up. Finally comes the seventh one, which is widespread destruction.

Many believe that the Tribulation period is the seventieth week of Daniel (Daniel 9:27), a "week" of seven years. If those judgments occur during that time, look what will happen with just two of them: With the fourth seal judgment, one-fourth of the population of the earth dies (Revelation 6:8). Under the sixth trumpet judgment, a third of the people left will be killed (Revelation 9:15). In other words, under just two of the judgments nearly half of the population of the world will be annihilated.

That is what Jesus meant when He said it would be great tribulation. Moreover, as the Tribulation proceeds, the judgments will be poured out with greater frequency. Unless the Tribulation is stopped, the entire population of the earth will be killed.

Is this not also what Jesus meant when He said that that time will be divinely interrupted for the elect's sake (Matthew 24:22)? It will be interrupted with the return of Christ to this earth. He will stop the judgment and put down all enemies under His feet. He will rule the nations with a rod of iron.

Why will God allow such a time as the Tribulation period to come upon the earth? One reason is to allow the program of Satan to run its course. That is why the restrainer, whom some interpret to be the Holy Spirit, will be removed during that time (2 Thessalonians 2:7).

Another reason is to deal with the nation Israel. That nation, which means so much to the Lord, needs to learn to trust Him. During the Tribulation, when Israel is so persecuted and afflicted, many will come to Christ. A third reason is to try the "earth dwellers" (Revelation 3:10), those who dwell on the earth, who have their lives wrapped up in the world. God must deal with sin, and He must deal with the sinner.

It is true that God is a God of love. But it is also true that God is a God of holiness, justice, and righteousness. As a holy and just God, He must judge sin. One day He is going to rule this world as He originally wanted it to be ruled. But man said he could do a better job. Throughout history we have paid the price for turning our backs on the Lord. One day, however, God will judge this world, will return, and will rule this earth in an age of righteousness. The nations today are being aligned for that purpose. Soon the judgment will begin.

What is the relationship of the church today to the coming Tribulation? Some believe that the true church, those who know Christ as their personal Savior in this age, will be taken out or raptured *after* the Tribulation period is over. That is called the *posttribulation* position. Others hold that the church will be raptured in the *middle* of the tribulation. It will, according to this view, go through the first half but be taken out before the events of the second half begin. That is called the *midtribulation* position.

There are many, however, who hold that the church will be snatched out, or raptured, *before* the events of the tribulation ever begin. That is called the *pretribulation* position.

Why do some believe the church will be raptured before the Tribulation begins? One reason is that the church has been promised to be kept from the wrath of God (1 Thessalonians 1:10; Revelation 3:10). Another reason is that the church is never seen in any of the Tribulation events. In fact, the word *church* is never used in Revelation 6-19, the chapters that speak of the Tribulation. Another reason is that the church is com-

manded to be looking for the return of Christ,
rather than for signs of the Tribulation. It is Israel
that will be on earth during the Tribulation, and
God gives her signs for the end of the age. On the
other hand, the church is to be looking for its
Savior from heaven (1 Thessalonians 1:10). Our
hope is the God from heaven (Titus 2:14), and our
deliverance is from heaven (Philippians 3:20).

As we see the way in which our world is staged
today, we cannot help but understand that it is
moving toward that day when the nations will
move against each other, judgments from God will
be poured out, and finally Christ will come to the
earth to set up His kingdom. But if the catching
away of the church is before that time, we may
well sense that that day is going to be very soon.
As we look at the events of the Tribulation period,
it will also help us to make sense out of which way
our world is headed. We need to be living our lives
in light of Christ's return for us. The current
events of our world will help us realize we may
have very little time left. Certainly if we meet the
Lord either by death or the rapture, our concern
must be to use every moment and opportunity of
service for Him.

We now turn to look at some of the events of the
Tribulation and the way our world is now headed.

5
The Cry for a World Leader

In a small rural town the men gathered for their regular Saturday night confab. They had finished their chores and dinner, and had hurried to the old country store. Sitting around the potbellied stove, they offered their solutions to the problems of the world.

"It's not right at all," began Joe. "Why is it we can't muster enough ambition to stand up to the other countries of the world? We keep being pushed around. I know I have to stand up to a horse or cow to make it mind. Why can't we do the same with other countries?"

It was Sam's turn next. "I remember when our country was the leader," he offered. "But we've lost a lot recently. Farming isn't what it use to be. I think it's our politicians."

"I remember when there were great leaders of the world," said Bob. "Maybe some of you do, too. Or you've heard your fathers talk about them. Winston Churchill. Now he had a way of moving people. Franklin Roosevelt did a lot for the country and the world. Douglas MacArthur was another. John Kennedy had a lot to offer, but his life ended too soon. And then there was Eisenhower."

"We have world organizations today, but they seem powerless. Look at the United Nations. And a lot is going on in Europe."

"None of us want the leadership of Russia," Jeff chipped in. "But at least they're strong. What we need today is a great world leader. Someone who can really take things in hand and solve our problems."

"Yeah, when I think of the Middle East," said Sam, "a world leader would be the answer. We need someone who could take those nations and really talk to their leaders. One who could sit down with them awhile, and make them understand."

"I agree that leadership is what it's all about," replied Bob. "But who could do it? Certainly there's no one qualified today. He would have to have charisma and intelligence. He would have to know people and the nations. He would have to be the leader of a whole empire. And he would have to have world support."

Charisma? Intelligence? World support? One day a leader who will have all of those will come on the world scene. He will lead nations and empires. He will lead world economies. He will support world religion. And he will fight and persecute the nations and peoples of the earth.

During end-time events, three persons will influence and lead this world. They will not be leading the world for good, however, but for evil. Their purpose will not be to make this world a better place for all, but a better place for themselves. All of us want leadership today for a good purpose. But one day leadership will be used for a bad purpose. It will be used to lead the world against the Lord of glory.

The time when those people will lead the world is called the Tribulation period. Many of the events at that time will be results of what they do. When they are at their zenith, Christ will return to the earth to stop their evil schemes and punish them. But until that time, during the Tribulation, they will show the world what happens when the world is left to run by itself, unrestrained by the Spirit of God.

In reality, there will be one leader, the Antichrist, who will lead this world against the Lord.

He will have with him a false prophet. That person will try to get the whole world to fall down and worship the Antichrist. He will work miracles to attract worldwide attention. And he will make the world wear the "mark of the Beast."

The one who will empower those two persons is none other than Satan himself. He will influence them and make them carry out his plans and purposes. He will get them to do what he wants them to do. And between those three evil persons, the world will be turned against the Lord from heaven.

Who is Satan? Although he has tried to deceive the world concerning his own existence, the Scriptures attest to his reality. Jesus talked about him on many occasions (Matthew 4:1-11, 16:23, 25:41; Luke 4), and he is mentioned in many other passages as well.

Satan originally was created by God as an angel, and was an anointed cherub (Ezekiel 28:13-14). He was privileged to be in the very presence of God until he sinned against the Lord of Hosts. Now it is his purpose to go against God and to do all he can to tear down what God is building up.

Jesus described Satan in very uncomplimentary terms. He said he was a murderer from the beginning and also a liar (John 8:44). Those are not nice characteristics, but they are true. Satan cannot be changed. He must always act according to his nature.

Satan's design is to counterfeit the plans, purposes, and program of God. When Satan sinned against God, he said in his heart five times, "I will" (Isaiah 14:13–14). He was trying to substitute his own will for the will of God. He was usurping the power and authority of the Lord Himself. He wanted to be *like* God, to be a counterfeit of Him (Isaiah 14:14).

That is seen in his appeal to Eve in tempting her to sin. He wanted to entice her to do evil by saying that if she sinned, she would be "like God" (Genesis 3:5). She would be part of his counterfeit system.

That is his appeal to the church today. He is not an angel of black or one dressed up in long, red winter underwear, with a pitchfork in his hand. Not at all. Rather, he is seen as an angel of light (2 Corinthians 11:15). He wants to be as acceptable as possible. He has his own plans and programs, which are anti-God. During the Tribulation period he will try to set up his own world government. He will try to use the Antichrist and false prophet to accomplish his goals. He will try to get the world to worship his people, the ones he will place in world leadership.

What is the doom of Satan? Although he is allowed, through the longsuffering of God, to mislead the world during the Tribulation, the Lord will bind him and cast him into the bottomless pit when He comes to set up His kingdom here on this earth (Revelation 20:3). After the thousand-year reign of Christ upon the earth (the Millennium), Satan will be loosed for a little while (Revelation 20:7). He will then be taken and cast forever into the lake of fire (Revelation 20:10).

The major human leader active during that time will seek to become the ruler of the world. He is known as the Antichrist, the one who is against God (1 John 2:18, 22; 1 John 4:3; 2 John 7).

The Old Testament prophets used many different terms to describe that man. For instance, he is called the "little horn" (Daniel 7:8). Daniel also describes him as wise and intelligent, one with great authority, and who has a kingdom that will devour the whole earth (Daniel 7:23).

He is also known as the "king of fierce countenance" (Daniel 8:23, KJV).* He is one who will destroy peace from the earth, stand against Christ, and eventually will be destroyed by the Lord from heaven. He is "the prince who is to come" (Daniel 9:26). He will make a covenant with Israel and will break it after three and a half years. He will exalt himself and speak against God. He will recognize no religion but his own. Although he will prosper during the Tribulation, his end will come.

How is he described in the New Testament? Jesus called him the "abomination of desolation"

*King James Version

(Matthew 24:15). One day, according to Christ, he will stand in the holy place, the rebuilt Temple, and there desecrate it.

The apostle Paul calls him the "man of sin" or lawlessness (2 Thessalonians 2:3). He will be identified after the rapture and will lead the world in great apostasy.

One of the most extended passages on this person is Revelation 13. There we find that he arises out of the sea, a reference to the nations of the earth (Revelation 13:1; cf., Isaiah 57:20). He is also "like a leopard, and his feet were like those of a bear, and his mouth like the mouth of a lion" (Revelation 13:2). Those animals are previously mentioned in Daniel as symbols of world empires of ancient history (Daniel 7:1–7). As Babylon, the lion empire, gave place to Medo-Persia, the bear empire, which gave place to Greece, the leopard empire, so it is that this beast will be the leader of a revived Roman Empire. This ten-nation confederacy will be one day assembled west of Israel.

Who gives the Beast, or Antichrist, his authority? It is Satan himself, known in this passage as the "dragon" (Revelation 13:2). Satan will be behind the Beast and will seek to get him to accomplish Satan's purposes.

What will the Beast do? First, he will be wounded to death and have that wound healed. Because of that miraculous display of power, the world will worship him. They will also want to

worship the dragon, or Satan, the one who gives
the Beast his power.

The Antichrist will rule for forty-two months, or
three and a half years, the last half of the Tribulation (Revelation 13:5). He will blaspheme God and
all those who dwell in heaven. His purpose is
anti-God and anti-Christ.

He will also make war with the saints, those
who are saved at that time (Revelation 13:7). He
wants to persecute the people of God. Those not
written in the Lamb's book of life will fall down to
worship him. They will be perverting what God
has put in their hearts for one who is against God.

The third person who will arise during the end-
time events will be the false prophet (Revelation
13:11-18). That leader is one who arises out of the
earth, or land, a reference to the land of Israel
(Revelation 13:11). Therefore, he is most likely a
Jew.

He also has two horns like a lamb and speaks as
a dragon. The fact he is like a lamb means he is a
counterfeit of Jesus Christ, the Lamb slain before
the foundation of the world (Revelation 13:8). In
that he speaks as a dragon means Satan, the dragon, gives him his authority and empowers him.
He, like the Antichrist, will be working the works
of Satan.

One of the major purposes of the false prophet is
to get the world to fall down and worship the Antichrist (Revelation 13:12). How does he do this?

One way is with great miracles. He will cause fire to come down from heaven in the sight of men (Revelation 13:13). That is what Elijah did in the Old Testament. This person will seek to imitate the power of God. He will use whatever means possible to get the people of the earth to fall down and worship the Beast.

He will also use the image of the Beast. He will make a huge image of the Beast and will have it animated so it will look lifelike. By being able to make the image speak, he will have a profound effect upon the world so the people will do as he directs.

In addition, he will cause all the world to receive a mark of the Beast (Revelation 13:16-17). The mark will be visible and will be on the right hand or forehead. It will have economic effects, for no one will be able to buy or sell without it. The number of the Beast is 666. Probably the best way to understand that is that six is the number of man. Man was created on the sixth day of creation, so that number represents man. The Tribulation and what this prophet will do is a result of man at his zenith. But God will come to stop that blasphemous time.

What will happen to the Antichrist and false prophet? When Christ comes to the earth to set up His kingdom, He is going to deal with them. He is going to take both of them and cast them alive into "the lake of fire which burns with brimstone" (Revelation 19:20). They will be tolerated by God so the world will see what will happen when there are no restraints and man is left to himself. But judgment is coming, and God will cast them both into eternal damnation.

Those are the leaders of the world during a yet future time. They will move the nations of the world to war against each other. Our world today is being so staged that it is now waiting for the rise of the Antichrist and false prophet.

But we need to examine what the Scripture teaches regarding the nations of the earth and how one day they will come together as they are moved by those end-time leaders. We now consider the end-time confederacies of nations and how our world is being shaped in light of them.

6
The Great Red Bear is Marching

It is marching! It is marching! The great Red Bear is marching!

With a vast number of troops and in lightning fashion, Soviet troops moved into Afghanistan. They shot the president, seized the capital, then fanned out throughout the country.

"Afghanistan is no more," lamented a bootblack in a shopping center there. "We have lost everything!"

For the last twenty years the Soviet drive for world domination has been stifled. There have been diplomatic pushes here and there, but world opinion, détente, and SALT negotiations have held them in check. But now, all of a sudden, the threat from the north has erupted again.

Russia's activities in Afghanistan, Iran, and Iraq may be but steps toward the Soviet Union's control of the oil supplies of the world. From Afghanistan she is only 350 miles from the straits of the Persian Gulf through which passes 40 percent of the world's oil supply. From Iran she can control the whole Persian Gulf and the oil fields of that country. That was the conclusion of President Jimmy Carter. "Soviet-occupied Afghanistan threatens both Iran and Pakistan and is a stepping-stone to their possible control over much of the world's oil supplies" (*Time,* 14 January 1980, p. 10).

Recent world events remind us of the shakiness of this age and the turmoil of the nations. The current situation shows there is the possibility of world military conflict, and many believe we are being hurled right into the very last days. The movement of Russia into Afghanistan and Iran is a signal. Many Bible students believe that when Russia moves into the Middle East, it may trigger the great war of Armageddon in fulfillment of Bible prophecy. The question is, are we witnessing today in the Middle East a foreshadowing of such an event? We can only wait and see.

There is underway a huge diplomatic and military buildup in the Arabian Sea, so the Middle East is becoming a fortress. The Soviet news agency *Tass* said recent events could lead "to a war in the Persian Gulf area" (*Chicago Tribune*, 26 April 1980). Many believe we are on the brink of Armageddon. What we are going to do for Christ needs to be done *now*.

Even though there is great uncertainty in our world, this is no time for the Christian to be uncertain. Rather, this is the time of opportunity, the time to demonstrate the meaning of the Christian life. The Chinese word for "crisis" consists of two characters. One character symbolizes danger, but the other means opportunity. Is it not true that when the night is the darkest the light needs to shine the brightest?

Before Christ returns to earth to set up His kingdom and rule the nations, four confederacies will surround the land of Palestine. One of those is a great northern confederacy that will come down against the land of Israel and there be destroyed by God. Is it possible that that northern confederacy is beginning to make its move?

Twenty-five centuries ago the Bible spoke of a day when a great northern confederacy would march into the Middle East. The prophet told how that would happen in Israel's "latter years," the time when she would exist as a nation and under world protection so she could dwell in "unwalled villages." Is what we are witnessing today the coming together of that confederacy and its predicted Middle East move?

What are the countries of the northern confederacy? Russia is a major one. In the vision of the prophet, God told him to set his face against "Gog of the land of Magog, the prince of Rosh" (Ezekiel 38:2). Although those names seem strange to us, Hebrew scholars such as Gesenius, Keil, and Lowth point out that the name *Rosh* (sometimes translated "chief") stands for the people of the modern nation Russia. Bishop Lowth wrote, "Rosh, taken as a proper name, in Ezekiel signifies the inhabitants of Scythia, from whom the modern Russians derive their name" (John Cumming, *The Destiny of Nations* [London: Hurst & Blackett, 1864], n.p.). The message then is against Gog, the symbolic leader of the land of Magog, that is, the prince of Rosh, or people of Russia.

Confirming evidence is that that confederacy will come from the "remote parts of the north" (Ezekiel 38:6, 15; 39:2). Would you believe that a careful look at a globe shows that the city of Moscow is nearly on the same longitude as the city of Jerusalem? Russia is therefore directly north of Israel.

What other nations will be confederate with Russia? One is Libya, an African state, far removed from Russia geographically but united with her in foreign policy ("Put," Ezekiel 38:5). Another nation is Ethiopia, also an African state, which not long ago was committed to the West but today is lined up with Russia (Ezekiel 38:5). A third country is Persia, which is none other than the modern country of Iran (Ezekiel 38:5). Although we wish there would be a time of peace in order to proclaim the Word of God, Scripture predicts Iran will be lined up with Russia as world end-time events come to a close. Could it be that what we are beginning to see is the alignment predicted by Ezekiel?

Why will the northern confederacy come against Israel? It is because of greed; it is to take a "spoil from the land" (Ezekiel 38:12-13). Throughout history great powers knew that the land of Israel was essential as they sought to expand their empires. That region was the nerve center of communications among three continents, a land bridge between Asia, Africa, and Europe. Alexander the Great understood that and made it the goal of his Grecian empire. The Caesars of Rome knew that and made it part of their empire. Is it any wonder that Russia should also want this "golden jewel"?

Russia also needs the area for self-preservation. All the Russian seaports in the Baltic Sea are frozen most of the year. If Russia is to have a warm-water port, it must be on the Black Sea or Persian Gulf. Russia needs to dominate the Black Sea, Mediterranean, Persian Gulf, and Middle East in order to protect her commerce.

Soviet intention to control the Middle East is clearly stated in Russian documents. The Ribbentrop-Molotov pact, signed in November 1940, agreed that "the area south of Batum and

Baku in the general direction of the Persian Gulf
is recognized as the center of the aspirations of the
Soviet Union" (Ira Hirschmann, *Red Star Over
Bethlehem* [New York: Simon and Schuster, 1971],
p. 56). Is it any wonder that Russia is on the
march?

Ezekiel says that Russia's coming is because of
the spoil of the land. Throughout the centuries
there has been great wealth in the Middle East,
such as agriculture in Egypt, dates in Saudi
Arabia, cedars in Lebanon. Why would a nation
with the natural resources of Russia want those?

That was the question until the discovery of oil.
All of a sudden, the Middle East took on an entirely new significance. Today the riches of the
world are flowing into the Middle East because of
the value and necessity of that precious commod-
ity, oil. In a day when the need for energy is so
great and energy is so unevenly distributed, the
nations that control oil control the world.

The largest oil producer in the world today is
not the United States, Saudi Arabia, Kuwait, or
the United Arab Emirates. Rather, the largest
oil-producing nation in the world today is the
Soviet Union (*Forbes,* 15 October 1979, p. 58). The
oil she does not use herself is supplied to the Eastern European nations, the Iron Curtain countries.
But Russia's oil is running out. New reserves are
not being discovered, and the wells presently
being drilled lie in western Siberia, which, be-

cause of weather and hazards of terrain, are difficult and expensive to drill. Moreover, Russia has problems conserving any additional energy. That is because she already has one of the most efficient rail transportation systems in the world. Russia is a nation with one automobile to every forty to fifty inhabitants, compared to the United States, which has one automobile to every two inhabitants. How can a modern industrialized nation conserve any more than that?

If Russia's oil is running out, where is she going to get more? The only obvious answer is the Middle East. Russia directly borders Iran, and if world opinion would allow, she could easily move into the Persian Gulf area and then into Israel.

Israel? Why would a world superpower be interested in a country smaller than the state of New Jersey? There are many reasons. One is that Israel may eventually have oil. Although only small amounts of petroleum have been discovered in the present land, some experts believe there may be oil in the marine shelf off Israel's Mediterranean shore. It is also possible that Israel's boundaries may change and encompass some oil fields. One day, during the Millennium, the tribe of Asher will "dip his foot in oil" (Deuteronomy 33:24).

Another reason is because of the Dead Sea. This body of water is one of the richest chemical beds in the world. It contains immense quantities of potash, bromine, magnesium, and other Dead Sea treasures. Potash is a nourishing fertilizer, essential for a nation like Russia that needs to import so much grain. Bromine is important in pharmaceuticals and gasoline, and Russia could use a lot of that. Magnesium is used in aluminum alloys, important in airplane construction. It is also used for war gases and the making of explosives. How important that would be for a nation wanting to fight a war.

But the Dead Sea offers something else. Israeli scientists have discovered in the water and salt flats the halophilic alga *dunaliella,* which can be converted into petroleum. It is possible that huge "oil farms" may develop in areas south of the Dead sea where the water could be channeled into salt-water ponds for the growing of *dunaliella.*

The Dead Sea also may produce huge amounts of electricity. In recent years, the water has been dropping due to the diversion of the Jordan's headwaters for farming. Experts envision a channel and tunnel arrangement that would pour the Mediterranean water into the Dead Sea (Harvey Arden, "The Living Dead Sea," *National Geographic,* February 1978, p. 230). That could become a major source of hydroelectric power, attractive to other nations.

Another reason Russia may want Israel is because of her strategic location. The control of Israel would provide Russia important military bases and control of the Mediterranean Sea. It would further provide the land bridge between the Middle East and Africa. Some believe Russia's purpose in spreading global Communism is to surround the North Atlantic Treaty Organization (NATO) nations by controlling the Middle East, Africa, and Latin America. Israel would be an essential link in such a plan.

There is another reason for Russia's interest in Israel. It is because of Israel's relationship to a great western confederacy. During that future time, Israel will be under the protection of a Western bloc of nations, nations that will be controlled by the Antichrist. A covenant will be made with Israel by this world-domineering confederacy, which will give religious sanctions to Israel for a short time (Daniel 9:27). Could it be that Russia would try to threaten such a great superpower by attacking its strategic protectorate, Israel?

Whatever the possibility for Russia's ambition and greed, few recognized the economic wealth of the Middle East and Israel until recently. Few, that is, except Ezekiel!

What will happen when Russia moves against Israel? When the northern confederacy comes down against Israel in the latter days before the return of Christ to the earth, a strange thing will happen. Instead of Israel's fighting and defending herself against Russia, God will utterly destroy that confederacy on the mountains of Palestine. God will rain upon Russia "an overflowing rain, and great hailstones, fire, and brimstone" (Ezekiel 38:22). There will be a shaking in the land so great that even the mountains will be thrown down and the steep places and walls will fall to the ground (Ezekiel 38:20). Civil war will break out, for every man's sword will be against his brother (Ezekiel 38:21).

Although there may be limited nuclear wars in the future, this judgment will come directly from God. The Lord Himself will destroy this nation because of her greed and selfishness, and because she came against His chosen people. Although God is a God of love, He is also a God of holiness, justice, and righteousness. He therefore must judge all who come against Him.

To see the devastation that can be brought by such disasters as earthquakes, volcanoes, and fire, I recently flew to the city of Pompeii, Italy. There I witnessed the utter desolation, the complete annihilation of a people that once inhabited that great city. "Why," I asked myself, "did all this come about?" The answer of history is clear. It is because of the sin, immorality, and pornography of the Roman Empire. Just as God destroyed the cities of Sodom and Gomorrah and the city of Pompeii, He will destroy a group of nations that will come against Him. How much better to know Him today as Savior than to stand before Him one day as Judge!

Why will God destroy the northern confederacy?

Ezekiel makes the answer plain. It is to magnify and sanctify the Lord. It is so He will be known in the eyes of many nations, "and they will know that I am the LORD" (Ezekiel 38:23). In other words, God's purpose then as now is to glorify Himself. It is to make Himself known throughout the world. And what God is going to do one day through the nations of the earth, He wants to do through us today. That is why uncertain times are no time for the Christian to be uncertain. Rather, they are a time to be demonstrating our faith before others. The amount of time we have before Christ returns is quickly evaporating. Should we not make every minute count for God?

7
World Power, World Problems

Throughout each month, 410 carefully elected people from nine European countries meet regularly to discuss the problems of the world.

First they meet in committees in Brussels, Belgium, and then in plenary sessions in Luxembourg and the brand-new "Palace of Europe" building in Strasbourg, France. There they debate the cost of agriculture, the production of industry, and the social benefits that accrue to their citizens. From their meetings decisions go out affecting most of the population of the world.

And what is the name of that select group? It is

the new parliament of the European Common Market!

The Common Market is rapidly becoming a world superpower. Already it is the world's largest trading bloc, importing and exporting more than the United States and the Soviet Union combined. It has a population of 270 million people and a gross domestic product almost as large as that of the United States. Declares France's Edgard Pisani, "This Parliament can have great political influence" (*Time*, 11 June 1979, p. 43).

But the Common Market has an important addition. The nine European nations are now expanded to ten. On January 1, 1981, Greece became the tenth member of the European Community.

As the Greek foreign minister put it, "From January 1, 1981, Greece will be an equal member of a huge democratic society of 270 millions— with a political voice equal to that of the major European powers in the decision making process" (Embassy of Greece, *Greece and the European Community*, Chicago, May 1979, p. 3).

From its inception, people such as Jean Monnet, the spiritual father of the Common Market, have always thought in terms of a ten-nation federation. And there are ten flag poles in front of the Common Market headquarters in Brussels, Belgium. As of January 1981 their vision is fulfilled.

More important, however, is that a Bible prophet long ago predicted there would one day come upon this earth a ten-nation federation in the approximate territory of the old Roman Empire. That western confederacy would play a strategic part in end-time events. A world empire would come against Israel and be involved in earth's final world war. Is what we see developing in Europe the fulfillment of the prophet's oracle? Are we witnessing the countdown to Armageddon?

The Scriptures predict that in the last days before the return of Christ to this earth there will be four great blocs of nations, four confederacies, upon this earth. One of those will be north of Israel, Russia and her allies, who will come against Israel and there be destroyed by God. We looked at that confederacy in the last chapter. The second major confederacy is west of Israel, a ten-nation federation. But if what is happening in Europe today is the formation of this western confederacy, we could well be standing at the starting gate of end-time world events!

What nations were to be in that western confederacy? We are not specifically told. But we do know many facts about the empire and what it will do.

For instance, we know there will be ten nations. The prophet Daniel spoke of the empires that would rise and fall upon the earth when he explained the wonderful image of Nebuchadnezzar's dream (Daniel 2). That image portrays the whole sweep of Gentile world history. Many Bible scholars agree that the fourth empire is Rome, which was at its zenith soon after the earthly life of Christ. Interest focuses especially on the feet and toes of the image, which we understand illustrate a reappearance or continuation of that great power.

Referring to the feet and toes, it is clear ten kingdoms make up this final Gentile power (Daniel 2:41-42). (The number *ten* is also mentioned in Daniel 7:7, 24 and Revelation 17:12, which support the previous passage.) Until recent times, however, no such ten-nation empire has appeared in that part of the world. But on January 1, 1958, six European nations banded together in what is today called the Common Market. Those nations were Belgium, West Germany, Italy, France, Luxembourg, and Holland. Fifteen years later, on January 1, 1973, the market was enlarged by Great Britain, Ireland, and Denmark. Since January 1981, for the first time in history, there have been ten members because Greece was admitted to full partnership.

But will the Community stop at ten nations? There is talk that both Spain and Portugal will soon join. But there is a lot of opposition to those nations' becoming full members. For instance, former French President Giscard d'Estaing recently said that the Community should not be expanded until current membership problems are resolved. He commented, "The community should give priority to completing the first enlargement before starting on a second" (*Chicago Tribune,* 9 June 1980). Of course, two members could go out of the Market and two others come in. But it is interesting in light of Scripture that there are now exactly ten members.

The western confederacy will be powerful. Daniel said that it would "be strong" (Daniel 2:42) and have great "dominion" (Daniel 7:26). In fact, it is not only to become *a* world power, it is to become *the* world power. "The fourth beast will be a fourth kingdom on the earth, which will . . . tread it down and crush it" (Daniel 7:23).

Up to now that prophecy has remained unfulfilled. No successor to the Roman Empire has ever achieved that kind of power. Through the centuries continental neighbors have quarrelled continually. Again and again disputes and rivalry have given way to bloody conflict. Twice in this century nationalism in Europe has flamed into global warfare.

Now, however, all of that has changed. Already the total population of the Common Market is greater than that of the United States. Soon their standard of living is expected to approximate that of our own country. This new confederacy may easily become the most powerful union economically, politically, and militarily, on the face of the earth.

Is it mere coincidence that a long-fragmented

continent, separated by different languages, cultures, histories, and traditions, should see the rise of a new federation? To find out what is happening, I visited the Common Market headquarters in Brussels, met with authoritative spokesmen, listened to facts and figures. My conclusion: Although there have been many problems, the new European Community is on the move.

Already they are the world's largest trading bloc. Their gross domestic product is growing. Their population is huge. They have negotiated commercial or association agreements with more than ninety countries. They have special trade and aid relationships with more than fifty former colonies in Africa, the Caribbean, and the Pacific. And all of that was before the addition of Greece.

That is why the National Security Council of the United States, in a special report, stressed the global effects of the Common Market. Their assessment:

"In the long run we could be confronted by an 'expanded Europe' comprising a Common Market of at least ten full members, associated memberships for the EFTA [European Free Trade Area] neutrals, and preferential trade arrangements with at least the Mediterranean and most of Africa. This bloc will account for about half of world trade, compared with our 15%; it will hold monetary reserves approaching twice our own; and it will even be able to outvote us constantly in the international economic organizations" (Henry Kissinger, *White House Years* [Boston: Little, Brown, 1979], p. 426).

It is also a political federation. There are only two ways to gain power: one is to take it by force, the other is by being given it. This kingdom will receive its power by mutual consent. "And the ten horns which you saw are ten kings, who have not yet received a kingdom; but they receive authority as kings with the beast for one hour. These have one purpose and they give their power and authority to the beast" (Revelation 17:12-13).

When we look at the Common Market, that is exactly what it purposes to be—a federation of states. Each nation maintains its individual identity, but has banded with the others for economic growth and protection. All the barriers to trade among member states have been torn down, whereas formerly each nation tried to post heavy tariffs on rival products and goods. A standard tariff is established on products coming into the Common Market from the countries outside of it.

Though the initial incentives to unity have been economic, leaders see the necessity for much more than that. " 'Political Union,' " says Professor Walter Hallstein, the first president of the Common Market, "is identical in meaning with the 'political unity of Europe' which the existing Community is designed to bring about and which its founders had in view as their ultimate goal" (Walter

Hallstein, *Europe in the Making,* trans. Charles
Roetter [New York: Norton, 1973], p. 293).

The idea of European unity is not new. In 1634
the Duc de Sully of France in his book *The Grand
Design* proposed a federation of European states.
In 1930 Aristide Briand advocated a European
federation of states to deal with tariffs, transport,
finance, health, social welfare, and technology.
Although nothing came of those early proposals,
the climate after World War II enabled the Common Market to be established with those hopes
and objectives in view.

Already there is the free movement of workers
between countries. Workers may seek employment anywhere in the Community, though gov-
ernments retain the right, in some cases, to re-
strict free movement of labor. Uniform European
Community passports have been introduced. The
passports bear the title "European Community"
above the national designation. There is also the
free movement of capital anywhere in the Community. Early leader Jean Monnet was given the
title "Honorary Citizen of Europe."

One important goal of European integration
was to establish a European parliament voted on
by direct elections instead of appointed members
as was done when the Market was first set up.
This step was taken when a European parliament
was directly elected in June 1979.

Another goal of European integration was to

have a common currency that would show political unity and make trade much easier. Such a European Monetary Union was first proposed in 1969, but enactment has been slow. The biggest move was taken in January 1979 when six of the countries created a new form of money, the European Currency Unit. That means that the money rates in those countries move up and down together.

Another mark of European integration is the establishment of a European postgraduate university in Florence. In addition, social programs, consumer protection programs, and environmental policies have been established.

The western confederacy will have a military purpose. The French government has announced the development of a neutron bomb which will soon be in production. Various Market leaders have spoken out on world affairs. At a meeting in Venice they endorsed Palestinian self-determination and urged that the Palestine Liberation Organization be included in Middle East peace negotiations.

"The major questions of the day are being decided by the superpowers," says Leo Tindemans, former premier of Belgium. "The Middle East, the source of our oil, the SALT signing in Vienna, raw materials. All these things are being done over our heads, and we Europeans must have a voice" (*Time,* 11 June 1979, p. 43).

Many believe it will be from this confederacy that the Antichrist will arise. One day he will make a covenant with the nation Israel to guarantee that nation protection (Daniel 9:27). But after three and a half years, he will break that covenant and move into the Middle East, even into the land of Israel (Daniel 11:41). It is then that he will lead his confederacy in earth's final world war, the campaign of Armageddon. Many in Europe seem ready for such a super leader.

The western confederacy will be in existence when Christ returns to the earth. Daniel wrote, *"And in the days of those kings* the God of heaven will set up a kingdom which will never be destroyed" (Daniel 2:44, italics added). The Lord of heaven will crush that confederacy and set up His own righteous kingdom upon this earth.

It is possible there may be changes in boundaries and nations in that confederacy before the return of Christ. But the fact is that never until now in the history of the world has there ever been a ten-nation federation in the approximate boundaries of the Roman Empire. If what we are witnessing is the formation of the long-awaited revived kingdom, how much longer will it be before Christ returns? We must ask ourselves, Will He find us using all the opportunities He has given us to minister to our world when He comes?

8
The Kings of the East

It is a land of contrasts, a land that defies the imagination.

It has one-fourth of the entire world's population inhabiting a mere 7 percent of its land area. It has thirteen of the fifty most populous cities of the world, one larger than Tokyo. It is the home of countless legends—of gun powder and hundred-year-old eggs, opium dens, and Buddhist pagodas.

And what is its name? It can only be China!

"China?" remarked the French general Napoleon Bonaparte. "There lies a sleeping giant! Let him sleep, for when he wakes he will move the world."

Although Napoleon lived many years ago, it is now that China is waking up. And as it does, it is starting to move the world!

People are visiting there in droves; over half a million tourists traveled to China in 1978. Businesses are anxious for the China trade. "China is the only market in the world big enough to fascinate us," says Assistant Commerce Secretary Frank A. Weil (*Newsweek,* 5 February 1979, p. 54), and well it is. China is expected to increase its trade with the United States from $1 billion in 1978 to over $7 billion by 1985.

China is also moving the world militarily. As China opens to Western peoples and industrialization explodes, there is a dramatic need for military preparedness. "People's war is good when the society is predominantly agricultural," explains an American expert. "As the society becomes industrialized, people's war means the sacrifice of the cities, and that means the sacrifice of the nation's security. As a nation develops an industrial base, it has to develop strength along the border to protect the industries" (*Newsweek,* 21 January 1980, p. 51).

It is for that reason that China, and much of Asia, is becoming militarily equipped. The threat of Russia, the lessons of Korea, Vietnam, and Iran, the protection of imported raw materials, have made those nations look to themselves for military defense. Already China has the world's largest army, many modern weapons, and nuclear bombs.

And who can say what advances it will make as it seeks to become a world superpower by the year 2000!

What is especially interesting is that Asian nations as large and important as China will figure predominantly in end-time world events. They are the ones that will march with great armies into the Middle East as world history climaxes. Are we therefore witnessing in the opening of China the formation of such an eastern confederacy?

Some believe China may be mentioned in Scripture as "Sinim" (Isaiah 49:12), one of the places from which Jews will be regathered to inhabit their land. But the major reference to China and other Asian nations who will march against Israel is as "the kings of the east" (Revelation 16:12).

You and I have lived through a time in which the nations of Asia have acted independently, and China was asleep as far as the rest of the world is concerned. But now as China is awakening and opening, nations of the east are coming together. Could we be witnessing the formation of "the kings of the east," an eastern confederacy that will have such a devastating effect upon the nations of the earth?

During end times, there will be four major groups of nations surrounding Israel. Two of those, the northern and western confederacies, we have already examined. The one we want to examine now, the eastern confederacy, is of special significance. It is the one that, when it invades the Middle East, will culminate the world's greatest war. Could the present awakening of China mean it will one day move the entire world?

Who are the kings of the east? Although exact nations are not mentioned, we are told they are nations from the east (literally, "from the rising of the sun") and beyond the Euphrates River (Revelation 16:12). Since the Euphrates River, which runs across Syria and Iraq, marked the eastern boundary of nations surrounding Israel, this must be a great Asian group of nations.

Certainly China fits such a description. Its sheer size, one billion people, makes it a major power of the world, let alone Asia. And now with its awakening, it is dominating more and more the Asian political scene.

The history of China has been long and involved with many bright periods, but Mao Tse-tung's Cultural Revolution made it exhausted. Now the Chinese hope is to become by the year 2000 a world economic and military power. From the opening of China in the early 1970s to normalization of diplomatic relations, China is now embarking on a New Long March or Four Modernizations program in an attempt to improve simultaneously agriculture, industry, science, and defense. Wrote the Peking *People's Daily,* "We are setting out to conquer on our New Long March the mountains, seas, plains, oilfields and mines of our motherland. We want to scale the heights of science and technology. We want to develop normal trade relations with other countries of the world" (*Time*, 1 January 1979, p. 13).

The Chinese have proceeded with ambitious vision. They have signed a seven-year, $13.5 billion trade and cooperation agreement with France. That includes two 900-megawatt nuclear power plants, which France will build at nearly $1 billion each. They have shopped in Britain, Denmark, Sweden, and the United States. They will get help in mining, fast-food techniques, communications. Inter-Continental Hotels plans to build a chain of 1,000-room hotels, complete with swimming pools and saunas. Hyatt International has proposed construction of hotels with a total capacity of 10,000 rooms. Pan American and other airlines are bidding for landing rights in China to bring in the tourist trade on a major scale. Much of that will be paid for with oil exports, oil that will account for 19 percent of China's foreign-exchange earnings by 1982.

The Chinese are taking crash courses in foreign languages. More than 1 billion copies of Radio Peking's English course have been sold in the capital. Some 10,000 Chinese students have been dispatched to study overseas. And all of that is revolutionary for a nation that for many years has been in the dark with respect to the rest of the world.

The Chinese are also building up their military. They have gone to Sweden, France, England, and the United States looking for modern weaponry to copy and with which to rearm their military forces. At present, China has the world's largest standing army (about 3.5 million) and the third largest navy (in terms of manpower). It has nuclear-powered submarines, missiles, and nuclear warheads. Warns a Western diplomat: "I wonder if an economically and militarily powerful China by the year 2000 would be an unmitigated blessing for American interests. Would a China strong enough to threaten Russia in nuclear terms not constitute any threat to us at all?" (*Time,* 1 January 1979, p. 19).

But there is more than one nation in this eastern confederacy, since the word *kings* in "kings of the east" is plural. Perhaps a second nation is Japan.

The economic advances of Japan are legion. All of us know the great strides it has made in steel production, semiconductor development, TV sets, communication equipment, and automobiles. And all of this for a country that imports close to 100 percent of its oil.

In order to protect industry and raw material supplies, Japan wants to build up its military forces. Under its present constitution, Japan cannot maintain armed forces for purposes of aggression. It does maintain national security by Self-

Defense Forces and has ships, aircraft, and military personnel. Most of the weapons have been supplied by the United States.

Recently, however, some in Japan have begun to lose faith in US military might because of Vietnam and Iran. For instance, political leader Yasuhiro Nakasone fears additional movements from Russia. "I am particularly interested in the statement of Dr. Kissinger," he says, "that the U.S. would not be able to fire an ICBM [intercontinental ballistic missile] at the Soviet Union, because it would mean mutual suicide" (*Business Week,* 31 December 1979, p. 54). Japanese Prime Minister Masayoshi Ohira warned, "The U.S. has become one of the powers and not a superpower any more. The days are gone when we were able to rely on America's [nuclear] deterrent" (*Business Week,* 19 May 1980, p. 67).

Others in Japan have begun calling for a defense buildup. They have suggested reestablishing the military draft and doubling present military expenditures. Some have urged a review of the country's ban on arms exports. One has warned that "Japan cannot forever be carried on the back of the U.S." (*Business Week,* 19 May 1980, p. 67).

In the midst of such moves for military independence, Japan has signed peace and friendship treaties with China and a trade agreement worth $20 billion. Japan will export steel and factories to China in exchange for Chinese oil. Is it possible that an eastern confederacy is now forming in that part of the world?

A third nation that may be part of the eastern confederacy is India. Many believe India to be a backward and poverty-stricken nation, but a careful study shows it has great potential economic and military strength. For instance, India now has the tenth largest national economy in the world. It is self-reliant in the manufacture of plants and equipment in major industrial sectors. It has the third largest pool of scientific and technical manpower after the United States and the Soviet Union. Oil-producing states in the Middle East are relying on India's engineering industry.

All of that has enhanced the country's military capabilities. It now produces small arms, ammunition, tanks, aircraft, rockets, and warships. It has the third largest army in the world (850,000) and an air force that has begun a $2 billion modernization program. Perhaps the most impressive development is India's nuclear research program. It produced its first nuclear explosion in May 1974. Improvements in the electronics and missile industries should make it possible to acquire an advanced nuclear capability by the mid-1980s. Even the United States recently offered India renewed nuclear assistance.

"But," someone may ask, "if it will take a few years for these nations to develop militarily, what makes them so important now?"

First is the sheer size of their armies and numbers of their peoples. China has the largest army and number of people on earth. Second is that that confederacy will have its greatest impact right before Christ returns to the earth, some seven years after the Tribulation begins. A lot of military development can happen in seven years. There is no question that the stage is set.

Why will those nations come together in a major world confederacy? One reason is economic necessity. Already there are signed peace and friendship pacts between some of the countries. Another reason may be religion. Atheism and Buddhism are important to those countries.

But the probable reason is their fear of the Soviet Union—the reason China opened to the world. Says Henry Kissinger, "Soviet and Chinese troops clashed in the frozen Siberian tundra along a river of which none of us had ever heard. From then on ambiguity vanished, and we moved without further hesitation toward a momentous change in global diplomacy" (Henry Kissinger, *White House Years* [Boston: Little, Brown, 1971], p. 171).

Japan is fearful of the Soviets. Because nearly 100 percent of its oil is imported, Japan fears its supplies could be cut off by Russia since Russia moved into Afghanistan. India is also fearful Russia could move into other middle Asian countries, including India. Although India has bought many supplies from Russia, it is now trying to diversify and is making defense commitments with France and other countries.

The three countries, Japan, China, and India are in a straight line headed right toward the Middle East. They with others could easily form a great eastern confederacy that will move against Israel.

Some may ask, "Why do we not see a political union of nations in Asia as we do in Europe?" We do not see it nor do we necessarily expect it. The Scripture points out that the western confederacy will be a federation of states, completely united together (Daniel 2:42; 7:24; Revelation 17:13). On the other hand, the eastern confederacy is made up of independent nations. They are "kings."

Their independence may be the reason they do not appear in end-time events until right before the return of Christ to the earth. It is during the Tribulation that the Antichrist will move into the Holy Land and set himself up as the world ruler. He will then go down to Egypt to take treasures of gold and silver. The kings of the east will allow the Antichrist to do so either because they are aligned with him or because of their own independence and internal problems. But finally, at the end of the Tribulation, they will amass a huge army. They will then invade the Middle East, war with the Antichrist, and be destroyed as Christ Himself returns (Daniel 11:44; Revelation 9:16; 16:12; 19:11-21).

From what direction will they enter the Middle

East? It is from the east, across the Euphrates
River that they will come. The river will be super-
naturally dried up to enable them to cross (Revelation 16:12).

The Euphrates River is the largest river of
western Asia, 1700 miles long. It rises in eastern
Turkey and flows across Syria and Iraq to the Persian Gulf. It is one of the four rivers said to be in
the Garden of Eden (Genesis 2:10-14) and is the
boundary of the land promised to Israel (Genesis
15:18).

Why do the Asian armies move across the Euphrates? One reason is that that area forms the
natural land bridge from Asia to the Middle East.
Another reason is that they could not come in
ships, for the Bab el Mandeb straits at the mouth
of the Red Sea are too small for the many ships
that would be required. But another reason is that
most of Iraq's oil is produced around the Euphrates.
By capturing those oil fields, the Asian armies
would ensure themselves enough fuel to wage war
against the Antichrist.

How large an army will the nations have? A
passage that gives the exact figure of this army
speaks of angels being loosed at the Euphrates in
preparation for war (Revelation 9:16)—200 million. Although that is hard to believe today, it is
possible those nations could quickly assemble that
many troops. In addition to having the world's
largest standing army, China has The People's

Militia, the members of which receive military training in their spare time. This military force is claimed to number 200 million, of which 75 million are women (*Encyclopaedia Britannica,* 15th ed., 4:294). That is not at all surprising when we consider that nearly 40 percent of the Chinese people—400 million of them—are under eighteen years of age. Certainly that number, 200 million, is not just a coincidence!

What will happen when this Asian army meets the Antichrist and his army? There will be the greatest war this world has ever seen. The nations of the earth will start to consume each other. Christ Himself will come from heaven and put all enemies under His feet. He, the King of all kings, will rule the nations with a rod of iron. He will establish peace and righteousness on the earth.

As we see the formation of an eastern confederacy, we need to ask ourselves some important questions. Are we making full use of our opportunities for God while we can? And, Are we involved in ministering to the peoples of Asia while we have time? Soon it will be too late!

9
Armageddon!

In January 1962, thirteen leaders of the Arab nations met in Cairo, Egypt, to plan what they would do when Israel began diverting the Jordan River for agricultural purposes.

Since that secret meeting there have been two major wars, much terrorism, and continued world conflict.

Now in spite of months of negotiation, peace accords, and Camp David summits, the Middle East is still a tinderbox that could be ignited at any moment. The scene shifts from Jerusalem to the Persian Gulf and back. It goes from racial hatred to oil. It moves from Israel, Egypt, and the Arab nations to the world superpowers.

But the startling fact continues to grip the people of our age: War is coming to the Middle East, and it is coming soon.

"All the masks have fallen and talk of peace with Israel has become a mere illusion," proclaims Crown Prince Fahd of Saudi Arabia, one of the most moderate Arab states and largest oil supplier to the free world (*Chicago Tribune,* 14 August 1980). His solution? A Muslim holy war against Israel.

The world, as never before, is prepared for an all-out conflict. The British have ships in the Persian Gulf area. The French have sizable bases, one at the mouth of the Red Sea. The United States has instituted draft registration and is training a $10 billion Rapid Deployment Force that could quickly move to any developing showdown in the oil fields. It also has vastly increased its presence in that area with ships, aircraft, and strategic bases.

"Our presence may be symbolic," says a White House aide, "but at least the countries there know that if the Russians come pouring over the border, we'll shoot at them" (*Newsweek,* 14 July 1980, p. 36).

The Russians? After what happened in Afghanistan, it is evident that the greatest military threat comes from Russia. That nation not only is strategically located directly north of Israel, but has overwhelming destructive potential. For instance, some estimate the Soviets now have 6,500 nuclear warheads operational in their strategic arsenal and could double that number by 1985 (*Aviation Week & Space Technology*, 16 June 1980, p. 67). With her own oil supplies running out, what would happen if Russia diverted oil from the West by either buying or seizing it? What would happen if oil to the industrialized world was cut off?

Jesus warned of coming war as a sign of the end of the age (Matthew 24:6). Other Scriptures predict a world-devastating war breaking out in the Middle East that will usher in the return of Christ. Is it possible that that is the event to which the nations of our world are rapidly stampeding?

Such signals from the Middle East should not worry us but remind us that our hope is not in this world but in the God who is sovereign over it. As we see the very foundations of our society crumble, we need more than ever to place our faith in our Lord. It is when we know where our world is headed that you and I can point a needy and frustrated people to the only Savior of mankind.

Sometimes this final world conflict is called "the battle of Armageddon." Although the place of Armageddon is involved, the Scriptures term this campaign "the war of the great day of God, the Almighty" (Revelation 16:14). It is a war, not just an isolated battle. It is made up of many battles, as was World War II or the war in Vietnam.

That conflict will be the war of "the great day of God, the Almighty." Even though men will fight each other, it is a war allowed by God. When nations come to the end of themselves, as they will in that conflict, God will bring it to an end. Fighting against heaven will be all mankind, but the Lord will be victorious.

Where will the war take place? Many Middle East oil nations think their land will be involved and have tried to protect it with the most sophisticated weaponry. That is true in Kuwait and Saudi Arabia, and even Iraq may have nuclear bombs. But the Scriptures predict that the center of the conflict will be Israel. For instance, one of the battlefields will be Armageddon, for it is there the nations will be gathered (Revelation 16:16). *Armageddon* is the Hebrew name for the Hill of Megiddo, located in the north central part of Palestine, between the Mediterranean Sea and the Sea of Galilee.

Megiddo was historically an important military garrison. As generals tried to take Israel, they knew if they controlled Megiddo, they could control the whole northern half of Israel. Why was Megiddo so important? It was because it was strategically located and had an underground springwater system so necessary for troops stationed there.

I flew to Megiddo to see its size and get a feel of its location. I climbed up on that hill, and when I did, I saw a huge valley, the Valley of Armageddon, which goes into the Valley of Jezreel, the largest valley in Israel. I then thought of Napoleon's remark when he stood there. He said, "This would make the most natural place for the nations of the world to be gathered for a final war."

There will be other battlefields for the conflict. One is the Valley of Jehoshaphat, located in central Palestine between the city of Jerusalem and the Jordan River. This today is called the "West Bank" area. God says, "I will gather all the nations, and bring them down to the valley of Jehoshaphat. Then I will enter into judgment with them there" (Joel 3:2). Could the present problems of the West Bank, the settlements and autonomy questions, be a prelude to the coming war?

Another place for that conflict is the land of Edom, or Idumea, in the southern part of Palestine. The Lord says His "sword is satiated in heaven, behold it shall descend for judgment upon Edom, and upon the people whom I have devoted to destruction" (Isaiah 34:5). It is believed that one day the people of Israel will seek to escape God's judgment by fleeing to the south (Revelation 6:16; 12:14). But even in that place there will be bloodshed.

The major place of contention, however, will be the city of Jerusalem. That city, whose name means "city of peace," has in its history seen many wars, even to the point of complete destruction.

But one day it again will be the center of conflict. God says, "For I will gather all the nations against Jerusalem to battle, and the city will be captured, the houses plundered, the women ravished, and half of the city exiled" (Zechariah 14:2). Could the problems of Jerusalem in our day be but the beginning of that future struggle?

In November 1977 President Anwar Sadat of Egypt made his famous trip to Jerusalem and there addressed the Israeli parliament. "The first thing we want," he said, "is the city of Jerusalem!"

Since that time there has been much negotiation about the Sinai, the West Bank, and the Gaza strip. But the problem of Jerusalem has been set aside until now it has become a time bomb, ready to explode!

The United Nations General Assembly recently voted for Israel to withdraw from the West Bank, Gaza, and East Jerusalem. Israel, on the other hand, affirmed that the united city of Jerusalem was the country's capital. Of making East and West Jerusalem one, Jerusalem's Mayor Teddy Kollek said, "Whom did it help? I see what confusion it has created, even among our friends" (*Time*, 11 August 1980, p. 30). Could it be that all of this is but the overture of the war to come?

How is the bloodshed of the conflict described? It is seen not as a harvest of souls, but as a harvest of God's wrath. An angel will thrust his sickle into the earth, gather the clusters from the vine, and throw them "into the great wine press of the wrath of God" (Revelation 14:19).

There will be a river of blood up to the horses' bridles, perhaps four and a half to five feet deep. It will cover two hundred miles (Revelation 14:20), the length of Palestine today. God confirms that the entire area of Israel will be covered with the blood of nations, from the north (the Valley of Megiddo) to the central (the Valley of Jehoshaphat and Jerusalem), to the south (the land of Edom).

What countries will fight in that final world war? During end-time events there will be four groups, or blocs, of nations that will surround Israel and come against her. Those confederacies are located in the north, west, east, and south of Israel. As we look at the world today, we can see that those blocs of nations already are formed. The stage is set for them to march!

The northern confederacy is Russia and her allies (Ezekiel 38-39). Those nations will come from "the north parts" as a "cloud to cover the land." Is Russia's moving into the Middle East a prelude of what the prophet predicted?

The western confederacy is a ten-nation federation located in the approximate area of the old Roman Empire. Carefully described in Daniel 2, it is the last part of the great image in Nebuchadnezzar's dream, which depicts the whole sweep of Gentile world history.

The European Common Market may fit the exact description given by the prophet Daniel. Beginning on January 1, 1958, it first was an association of six nations. But now, with the addition of Greece, for the first time it consists of exactly ten nations. Could it be that this confederacy, with its European parliament, is being readied for the end-time events predicted by Scripture?

The eastern confederacy is east of the Euphrates River and Israel and is called "the kings of the east" (Revelation 16:12). China, Japan, and India with other nations may make up that confederacy. Are the overtures between those nations preparing them also for coming war?

But who is the southern confederacy? Could that be where the Arab nations fit in?

Although it is true the Arab states will support the southern nation, there never has been any great unity among the Arab countries. Arabs have spent more time fighting each other than in finding avenues for cooperation. And in prophecy, God has different purposes for the Arab nations.*

Who, then, is the southern nation? The Scriptures point out it is the country of Egypt, called "the king of the south" (Daniel 11). Although Arab states may periodically support this country, the word *king* is singular and shows that Egypt acts alone. Is that not true today?

Egypt is a country with limited resources and

*For a further understanding of the future of the Arab nations, see Edgar C. James, *Arabs, Oil and Energy* (Chicago: Moody, 1977).

overpopulation. It is a nation of 38 million people, most of whom live in extreme poverty. The government uses 50 percent of its revenue to subsidize basic commodities. The nation is dependent on the handouts of others just to keep going.

Although Egypt is not a leader economically, she is a powerful leader politically. She is the one who began the peace process. She is the one who obtained land through negotiation. And she is the one who could upset the whole easing of tensions in the Middle East.

How will the final war begin? In a most illuminating passage God tells us exactly what will happen. At the "time of the end" Egypt, the "king of the south," will come against Israel (Daniel 11:40). Her pushing against Israel, an agitation that will start the conflict, will cause the northern confederacy to come down against Israel.

Why will Egypt come against Israel? Some may speculate it is because of oil, but Israel has very little oil. It may be because of Egypt's not getting her way during peace negotiations. She could easily break off talks with Israel over an issue like Jerusalem, as she has already done.

But the underlying reason is the Arab's continued hatred of the Jew, and it is only God who can change that. Speaking of the Arab nation Edom, the Lord says she has "everlasting enmity," or a "perpetual hatred," of Israel (Ezekiel 35:5). The psalmist confirms that hatred. The Arab nations have said, "Come, and let us wipe them out as a nation, that the name of Israel be remembered no more" (Psalm 83:4). They have also "conspired together with one mind" (Psalm 83:5). Is that not happening today?

What will take place after Egypt pushes at Israel, giving Russia the excuse to come against that nation? It is then that God will destroy those northern armies on the mountains of Palestine (Ezekiel 38–39).

Until that time, there will have been a balance of world power. But when the northern armies are destroyed, the western confederacy, the revived Roman Empire led by the Antichrist, will move into the "Beautiful Land" (Daniel 11:41). That bloc of nations will take the treasures of the land, including the "precious things of Egypt" (Daniel 11:43). That is also the time when the Antichrist will put himself in the rebuilt Temple and call himself god (2 Thessalonians 2:3-4).

What will be the climax of that war? The western confederacy, threatened by the kings of the east, will come out of Egypt back to the Holy Land to fight the eastern confederacy (Daniel 11:44). But instead of fighting each other, their hatred is turned against the Lord from heaven, who comes and slays His enemies (Revelation 19:21). The City of God will win, as Augustine said, and Jesus Christ will be victorious!

The hope of the world is not in the nations of the

earth or in this world itself. Rather, the only hope of this world is in the Savior from heaven, who one day is coming to bring in an age of righteousness and rule the nations with a rod of iron. As Nebuchadnezzar learned, "the God of heaven will set up a kingdom which will never be destroyed, and that kingdom will not be left for another people; it will crush and put an end to all these kingdoms, but it will itself endure forever" (Daniel 2:44).

If it is the Lord who is going to win, should we not be working for Him and doing His will today? And should we not be witnessing to the people of this whole world before it is too late?

10
The United States and Other Nations in Prophecy

It is a land of majestic hills and lush green valleys. It is a country of tall skyscrapers and mile-high cities. It is a place of technological advances and creative people. It is the United States of America!

"Give me your tired, your poor, your huddled masses yearning to breathe free," counsels the

Statute of Liberty as she holds out her torch to the thousands from around the world. And they have come, in droves, to this "land of opportunity."

But now the country is having problems, and the people face frustration. Inwardly there are struggles in productivity, inflation, and morality. Outwardly there are threats from other nations. "America must be great again," politicians proclaim. And the people say, "We need to lead the world!"

But where is the United States going? What is the future of this great country? Where do America and other nations fit into Bible prophecy?

As we approach end-time events, four confederacies of nations will surround the land of Israel. Is it possible the United States will be aligned with one of those confederacies? Or will she dominate the world, or perhaps be destroyed? Does the Bible say anything about the future of the United States?

Some, in reading Scripture, believe various passages may allude to the United States. But such conclusions are very remote. For instance, some hold the "young lions" (Ezekiel 38:13; KJV) and "islands" (Psalm 72:10) refer to England's colonies, namely America. But a careful check shows those are villages or islands of Tarshish, the area of southern Spain (cf. Jonah 1:3).

Others find America as the "great eagle" (Revelation 12:14) or the "land shadowing with wings"

(Isaiah 18:1, KJV). But the Revelation passage is showing the speed with which the woman flees into the wilderness, not a nation. The Isaiah passage refers to a nation with "whirling wings" (Isaiah 18:1), most likely a reference to the insects of Ethiopia.

Still others find America destroyed in the judgments poured out during the Tribulation (Revelation 6:8; 8:7), or as part of the 144,000 that will come upon the earth during that time (Revelation 7). But the judgments in Revelation are upon the "whole world" (Revelation 3:10), not just on one part of the world or one nation. Moreover, the 144,000 are a limited number of saved Jews that will be special evangelists during that time (Revelation 7:3–4). How can the United States as a nation qualify for that biblical description?

To say the United States is not mentioned in Scripture, however, does not mean this nation will be destroyed. The Bible is discussing the nation Israel and what will happen around that nation during end-time events. Since the United States is not anywhere near Israel, it is not mentioned. That is not surprising since no other nation in the Western Hemisphere or Australia is mentioned either.

What will happen to the United States? Certainly we can assume that when Russia comes down against Israel to take the "spoil of the land" (Ezekiel 38–39), the United States will oppose it.

Could that be why the United States has taken such a position against Russia today?

During end times there also will be power shifts to the Middle East and the confederacies that surround Israel, especially the ten-nation revived Roman Empire. Already such power shifts have begun.

You and I are witnessing the greatest redistribution of wealth in the history of the world. Billions of dollars from the industrialized nations are pouring into the Middle East to buy oil. Japan imports nearly 100 percent of its oil. Europe buys much of its oil, and the United States imports a great deal of its oil from the Middle East. The OPEC (Organization of Petroleum Exporting Countries) nations are rapidly accumulating the vast wealth of the world. Whole cities are being built in the desert because of their money, and sophisticated weapons are making that part of the world a military fortress. Already we are seeing our standard of living suffer and many armed conflicts in the Middle East.

There also are power shifts to the confederacies that will surround Israel in end-time events. The present fear of Russia shows its domination. The opening of China and its economic plans is the beginning of a shift to the "kings of the east." The leadership of Egypt in its relationship with Israel and the Arab world is markedly different than it was twenty years ago. And the rise of the ten-nation Common Market is surprising when viewed against the fragmented history of European nations.

Since those power shifts are already beginning, why is it the United States is still the dominant country of the world? Why is it that this country continues to exert such vast world leadership?

Perhaps the answer lies in its technological achievements. But other countries, such as Japan and West Germany, have made great strides in technology but do not exert the world leadership as does the United States. Perhaps it is our political system. Yet there are other countries, like England, Canada, and Australia, that have strong political systems, but do not have the influence of the United States.

On the other hand, when we look at the moral condition of this country, we get a very pessimistic picture. When we look at America's sin, in every level of society, we ask, "Why is it that God has not judged this nation?" When we look at the breakdown of the family, abortion, homosexuality, drugs, we ask, "Why is America a leader at all? Why has there not been more of a power shift than what has already started?"

Centuries ago the Bible spoke to this very issue. Within its pages it tells the secret for national success. Because America has followed those basic principles, we live in the greatest nation on earth. But will the dominance of this country continue?

Or are the power shifts now beginning going to crescendo in the days ahead?

All the biblical principles for national survival are strategic. First is the importance of righteousness. God clearly says it is righteousness that "exalts a nation, but sin is a disgrace to any people" (Proverbs 14:34). This principle is also expressed by the psalmist who said, "Blessed is the nation whose God is the LORD" (Psalm 33:12).

History records this nation was founded on basic biblical principles—it was founded on righteousness. From our coinage which says, "In God We Trust," to our pledge of allegiance, to the Constitution, religious freedom was the hallmark of this nation.

But today we are getting away from our founding faith. And as God says that "sin is a disgrace to any people," He easily could destroy this nation because of its sin. Did He not do that with Sodom and Gomorrah (Genesis 18–19) and the nations of Canaan (Deuteronomy 9:4–5)? How important it is for our nation to get back to God's righteousness!

There is another reason that God has blessed this nation. It is because of our relationship to the Jew. God told Abraham He would "bless those who bless you, and the one who curses you I will curse" (Genesis 12:3). Although some claim that that promise has gone out of existence, they freely admit that the promise of the rest of the verse, that "in you all the families of the earth shall be blessed," continues. Certainly then, God's blessing for those who bless Irael continues as well.

Throughout the history of the United States, this nation has been very kind to the Jewish people. We have provided a haven here for many of the seed of Abraham. Jewish people have come to this country so they could worship in religious freedom. Many have found unusual opportunities in government, business, and communications. Although judgment on other countries sometimes has been preceded by persecution of the Jew, in this nation Jewish people have had the same treatment as everyone else.

We also had an important place of leadership in helping found the state of Israel in 1948. Although not everything the state of Israel has done has been right, the United States has consistently been on the side of helping that nation and working with it. In recent times this nation has come to the aid of Israel when other nations were calling for its removal from the United Nations.

But with the world oil problems, will the United States continue to treat equally the Jewish people and back the state of Israel? We certainly need oil since we import so much from the Middle East. We also need the friendship of Arab peoples, and the Bible promises they also have a future under the hand of God (Isaiah 19:19–25). But as a nation we dare not move away from our support of the Jewish people or the state of Israel, even though there may be honest differences between two sovereign states. Until our Lord returns, we need to continue genuine support for this people.

Perhaps the most important reason God has blessed this nation is because of the church. It is during this age that God is building His church, saving people, and adding them to the Body of Christ (Matthew 16:18). The reason the Lord has not as yet returned for His church is that it is not as yet complete. He has delayed His coming so that many in this age will be saved (2 Peter 3:9,15). During this time of God's program, the building of His church takes precedence over dealing with the affairs of nations. One day, however, the church will be complete, and He will return for it.

The church in the United States has had a large part in being the instrument God has used for bringing people to Christ throughout the world. The United States, with only 7 percent of the world's population, has produced over 50 percent of the manpower and money for world missions in the last century. (Since 1950 it has produced nearly 70 percent.) Many of the biggest and most influential missionary organizations, both denominational boards and non-denominational "faith" groups, are headquartered in the United States. In its history Moody Bible Institute alone has trained over 5,600 people who have gone to foreign fields with the gospel.

From the human side, because of the moral degeneracy of our nation, we may wonder why it is God has not as yet judged this nation. But from the divine side, when we look at what God is doing through the church both here and around the world, we can see why God's hand of blessing has been upon this nation.

One day, however, the Lord is going to come to take His true church, all those who know Christ as their own personal Savior, out of this world. Jesus said, "I will come again, and receive you to Myself; that where I am, there you may be also" (John 14:3). Jesus Christ is coming again, and He is coming for His church!

What will happen when the Lord takes all true believers to be with Him? What will happen when God removes the church from the United States? No longer will there be the penetration of society with the gospel. No longer will there be restraint from sin. No longer will righteousness exalt this nation. No longer will this nation support the Jew. And no longer will there be a world missionary enterprise led and supported by the church in this country.

All of a sudden, with the church gone, this nation will become as any other nation. All of a sudden this country will be as any other group of people.

It is possible that after Christ comes for His church, this nation will be destroyed. It is more likely, however, that this nation will become an associate nation with one of the confederacies surrounding Israel in end-time events, probably the western confederacy that will be led by the Antichrist. It is that confederacy that will "devour the whole earth" (Daniel 7:23) so that no nation, including this one, can be kept in complete isolation from those events. As a result, the United States probably will be associated with that confederacy since throughout history our national ties have been closely connected with Europe.

With the church gone there will be a complete power shift to the nations of the Middle East and the confederacies that will surround Israel. No longer will the United States be a world power. Rather it will be set to play its part in end-time events, supporting the man of sin and eventually moving against Israel and the nations of the world in the war of Armageddon. It is then that Christ will come to the earth and put all enemies under His feet, including His enemies in this country. It is then He will judge the nations of the world, including this one. And it is then He will rule the nations with a rod of iron, and of His kingdom there will be no end.

You and I need to be involved in God's program for this age, that of building His church. Already there are power shifts beginning, power shifts to the Middle East and power shifts to the confederacies that will surround Israel. One day God will be dealing with those nations and moving them to carry out His purposes. But until He takes us out of this world, His purpose in this age is saving people, not building nations. Should this not be our purpose as well? Soon it will be too late.

11
The Hope of the World

"It was a five-alarm fire," the officer told me. "I've never seen anything like it. And to think it was a school. Bodies were charred beyond belief. It was a terrible thing. How the families must have suffered."

I had heard about the fire, and the grade school, and how many of the children could not get out. It happened so quickly. The firemen came. The crowds gathered. But no one could help the eleven little lives that were lost.

Now over a year had passed, and every day, in

hot and cold, rain and snow, a woman walked to that vacant site. She came, generally with flowers in her hand, and would kneel for a moment of silence by the few bricks that remained. Each time I passed by, I saw her do the same thing.

Finally, I got up enough nerve to speak to her. "Why do you come here each day?" I asked. "There's nothing here. The fire was over a year ago. All that is here now is a vacant lot."

"I come because my son was one of those who may have died in that fire," she said. "But he may not have died. The bodies could not be recognized, you know. He may not have died. I come because I still have hope!"

Everyone has some kind of hope. Some hope for a better job. Others for better opportunities, many for a better life. Some hope in the midst of tragedy. Without hope, life has no purpose.

Throughout history many have hoped for a better world. Some wanted a Utopia, a place where everything would be perfect. Arab legends looked for a city in the Atlantic, or western ocean. But when we view all the problems we face today, many ask, "How can we have hope?"

Poverty and suffering are on every hand. How can they be removed? How can war be be eliminated? When we look at our world, it is getting worse, not better. Our standard of living is falling apart. Our moral conditions are shocking.

Some believe those problems will be solved by science. Others believe money is the answer. Still others believe that the creativity of man is the best way to improve. But as yet, none of those has moved the world toward any of those goals. Nor will they.

Man himself must be changed before his society can be changed. There must be a new heart within, a change from the inside out. It is by regeneration, not reformation, that answers are brought to the problems of life. One day God will bring into being His own perfect world, His glorious kingdom here upon this earth. Not until then will those goals be realized, and no counterfeit method by man will speed the reality.

What will happen when Christ returns to this earth? The apostle carefully describes His coming. He arrives on a white horse, white being the symbol of purity (Revelation 19:11). He is called "Faithful and True," the one who alone is consistent and conforms to reality. It is in righteousness that He will judge and wage war. That is how He will put all enemies under His feet.

How else is He described? He has eyes as a flame of fire, showing His discernment and omniscience (Revelation 19:12). On His head are many diadems, for He is the sovereign of the earth. His robe is dipped in blood, which not only shows His redemption for sin but His coming judgment upon the earth. His name is called "the Word of God"

(Revelation 19:13), for He is the manifestation of God Himself.

Who will come with Him when He comes to the earth? Following Him from heaven will be His armies, the saints of God who already have been rewarded by Him. He will smite the nations with His sharp sword (Revelation 19:15), and He will rule them with a rod of iron. He will tread the winepress of the fierce wrath of God.

What is the name of this one who comes like this? Both on His robe and on His thigh, the place of strength, He has a name written, "KING OF KINGS, AND LORD OF LORDS" (Revelation 19:16). He is the King of all kings and the Lord of all lords. He is the one who not only has authority to rule, but will also use that authority in ruling this world. Jesus Christ is coming again, and He is coming to set up His righteous kingdom upon this earth.

What will the reign of Christ be like? It will be unlike anything of which we know today. First, it will have a political arrangement. That has many implications. For instance, it will be an earthly kingdom. It will be a display of God's authority over the earth (Psalm 2:8).

When God made this world, He intended to rule it, but He gave man the privilege of choice. Man said he could do a better job, and usurped the authority God had over this world. Man wanted his own human government, with kings and rulers and leaders. But he has found that does not work. One day Christ himself will be the king and rule this world as God intended it to be ruled.

During that future time Jerusalem will be exalted among the cities of the earth (Isaiah 2:2-3; Micah 4:1-2; Zechariah 14:10). That is why the city of Jerusalem is in such contention today. One day it will be the chief among the cities of the earth, and the nations of the world will stream to it. During that time many people will say, "Come, let us go up to the mountain of the LORD, to the house of the God of Jacob; that He may teach us concerning His ways, and that we may walk in His paths" (Isaiah 2:3). It is from Zion, the city of Jerusalem, that the law and word of God will go forth to the whole earth.

It is at this time that God will judge the nations. His judgment will be righteous and His decisions just. Immediate acts of sin will cause people to be cut off immediately. It will be a time of peace. Swords will be hammered into plowshares, and spears into pruning hooks (Isaiah 2:4). The weapons of war will be turned into implements of peace. Nations will not lift up swords against nations anymore, nor will they learn war.

Who will rule with Him? During the millennial kingdom there will be many spheres of authority, as is true today. We have senators, representatives, presidents, who all have different spheres of authority. So it will be in the future. Jesus Christ will be the center of His rulership. But others will serve with Him.

The church will rule with Him, princes will also rule (Isaiah 32:1), elders will come forth from them (Jeremiah 30:21). Princes and those over the people will have an important place (Ezekiel 45:8-9).

Where will Israel be during that time? That special nation chosen by God will be the subjects in the king's reign (Isaiah 9:6-7). They will be in the kingdom and pay allegiance to Christ. They also will be exalted above the Gentiles (Isaiah 14:1-2; 61:6-7). Gentiles will attach themselves to the house of Jacob, but Israel will rule over them. Israel will be called the priests of the Lord, and will eat the wealth of the nations. Instead of shame, they will have a double portion from the Lord during that time. God's hand will be upon them.

Israel also will be special witnesses of God. They will be speaking forth as ministers of the earth (Isaiah 61:6). They will be like dew from the Lord giving forth His word (Micah 5:7). They will be blessed by the Lord as they serve Him.

What will happen to the other nations of the earth? They also will share in the economic and spiritual blessings of God in that time. They will be subordinate to Israel (Isaiah 14:1-2; 49:22-23; 61:5-9). But they will be in the land and will be provided for there.

Where will Satan be during that time? He is the one who will empower the Antichrist during the Tribulation period. But during the Millennium he will be bound and placed in the bottomless pit (Revelation 20:1-3). He will not be destroyed; later he will be cast into the lake of fire (Revelation 20:10).

At the end of the Millennium, Satan will be loosed from the bottomless pit for a little while. During that time he will incite those who have been born in sin during the Millennium. He will seek to get them to move against God (Revelation 20:8). Even during such a perfect age as the Millennium, man left to himself will sin against God. But then God will take Satan and cast him into the lake of fire.

What will the spiritual life be like during that time? Since Christ will be reigning, His glory will be manifested (Psalm 72:19). The whole earth will be filled with His glory. There also will be increased knowledge during that time. The entire earth will be full of the knowledge of the Lord (Isaiah 11:9). The whole world will know the Lord, from the least to the greatest of the people on earth (Jeremiah 31:34). No longer will people need to be taught by the Lord, for already they will know Him.

Righteousness will prevail. God's righteousness will flourish (Psalm 72:7). Righteousness will be the belt about His loins (Isaiah 11:5). People will not make judgments according to what is apparent, but rather the Lord will judge righteously.

Another mark of that time will be the joy that will come to the people of the earth. It will not be a synthetic joy, but a real joy out of grateful hearts. They will joyously draw water (Isaiah 12:3). They will be giving thanks to the Lord (Isaiah 12:4). They will shout for joy over their portion (Isaiah 61:7). It will be an exciting time because the people will be serving the Lord.

One of the greatest marks of that time will be the outpouring of the Holy Spirit upon the world. God promises that He will pour out His "Spirit on the house of Israel" (Ezekiel 39:29). He promises that when that occurs the people will prophesy and dream dreams (Joel 2:28–29). Although the Holy Spirit today is present in all believers, during that age there will be a special outpouring of Him.

People also will be saved during the Millennium, although it will begin with only saved people entering it. That is because the wicked will have been purged out (Ezekiel 20:33–39; Matthew 25:31–46; Revelation 19:11–21). People will have natural bodies and bear children, and the people born will, as in every age, be born in sin. But as the kingdom begins, it will be a time of righteousness. During the kingdom age, as people are born, when they commit great acts of sin, God will immediately judge them and cut them off. Jesus

Christ will rule in righteousness, and He will judge sin immediately.

The earth itself will be affected. The curse will be partially lifted, and the earth will blossom as a rose (Isaiah 35). There will be abundant rainfall, a sign of blessing of God upon the earth (Isaiah 30:23; 35:7). There will be enough food and cattle for the whole earth (Isaiah 30:23-24). No longer will famine be the order of the day. It is then that the lamb and the wolf will lie down together, showing the peacefulness of the age (Isaiah 65:25). It is evident that the curse will only be partially lifted, for people will still be born in sin and some will die (Isaiah 65:20).

There will be general prosperity during the Millennium. The land will produce plenty (Ezekiel 34:25-27; Joel 2:21-27; Amos 9:13-14). There will be just compensation for work then done upon the earth (Isaiah 65:21-25; Jeremiah 31:5).

During that time there also will be abundant health and healing, a mark of God's grace and blessing upon this world (Isaiah 29:18; 35:5-6; 61:1-3; 65:20; Jeremiah 30:19-20; Ezekiel 47:22).

God's way is always the best way. One day Jesus Christ is coming to this earth to rule it. When He does, it will be a time of righteousness, peace, prosperity, and blessing. The answer to the struggles the world is now facing is the return of Christ.

What should we be doing until our Lord returns? We need to preach the gospel to the world and be witnesses of the changed lives we have. It is as others see us demonstrate the life of Christ that they will accept God's provision for them. When they do, they also can look forward to the time when Christ returns, first for His church, and then to set up His kingdom upon this earth and rule it in peace.

12
What Happens When We Die?

It happened when Sarah was a freshman in college. She tried to adjust to her new life—the studies, the social scene. But six weeks into the semester it hit her like a ton of bricks.

"We need you home right away," her mom said on the phone. "Grandpa just died, and the funeral will be Friday. Catch the next plane home, and we'll meet you at the airport!"

The funeral was beautiful but difficult. All the relatives were there, so it was good to see everyone. Grandfather was well known and respected. He had lived a good life and had now entered his final rest.

As everyone left the house after the funeral, Sarah went to her room to think. She had thought about death many times. But now it became personal and hit her very hard. "Where is Grandfather now?" she thought. "What really happens when we die?"

No one wants to die. Yet the Scripture says it is "appointed for men to die once and after this comes judgment" (Hebrews 9:27). Although no one looks forward to death, this subject is the one people think about almost more than any other. Death is coming for all of us, and it is important that we be prepared.

Is death the end of life? What really happens after we die?

Throughout history there have been many views concerning life after death. For instance, the Egyptians believed their kings in the next world would live much as they did here. As soon as a king began his reign, his people would begin building his tomb. When he finally died, all of his earthly possessions would be buried in the tomb with him.

Others believed, however, that death was the end of all things, the cessation of existence. This life is all there is; there is no life after death. Such a view is in conflict with Scripture, which teaches that all will be raised to eternal existence one day (John 5:28–29).

Still others believe in soul transmigration, the view that after death, the immaterial nature of the person goes into another person or even an animal. Sometimes this is called reincarnation. The person is said to come back as someone or something else. But again there is no scriptural basis for such a view. The Bible always shows each individual to be personally responsible after death (Luke 16; Revelation 4). He does not float from body to body.

Some hold to conditional immortality. This view holds that those who have done good works in this life will have a life after death. Those who have done wicked works, however, will not have a life after death. In other words, those who have lived good, noble, and moral lives will receive their reward by living after death. Those who have not lived such good lives will cease to exist after death. But again there is no Scripture to support this view. Jesus said that even the wicked will be raised (John 5:28-29). And, how can not living be an adequate view of future punishment for one who has been wicked all his life?

Another view sometimes offered is universalism, the view that everybody will be saved. Everyone will live forever in the same place and for the same purpose. But again that view is in conflict with Scripture. The Bible teaches that there is a heaven and there is a hell. Not everybody will be saved. Only those who have trusted Christ as their own Savior from sin will live with Him forever.

There are many reasons why people believe there is life after death. One reason is so that moral aspirations of people can be fulfilled. Many have moral aspirations that never can be fulfilled in this life. Does it not make sense that there must be a life in which those aspirations will be fulfilled?

Another reason is because of the nature of rewards. Have you ever considered how a person who has been wicked all his life can truly be punished? Or how can a person who has done great and noble things all his life truly be rewarded? For instance, what about a man who kills thirteen people? Although he is tried and convicted of murder, he can die only once for that particular crime. He cannot die thirteen times. How, then, can he truly be punished for such behavior? The only answer is that there must be life after death. There must be future existence in which people are properly punished or rewarded.

The best argument for future existence, however, is in the Scriptures. Throughout the Bible God shows that we will be resurrected from the dead and there is life after death. That is the teaching of the book of Job, probably the oldest book of the Bible. Job not only knew that his Redeemer lived but also that "from my flesh I shall see God; whom I myself shall behold, and whom my eyes shall see and not another" (Job 19:26–27).

An Old Testament prophet who taught there

was life after death was Daniel. He said that Israel would come forth from the grave (Daniel 12:1-2). The prophet Isaiah also spoke of life after death (Isaiah 26:19).

Probably the greatest teaching on life after death comes from the New Testament. Jesus said that not only had all judgment been committed to Him, but that He was the source of the resurrection life as well. One day, He said, all "who are in the tombs shall hear His voice, and shall come forth" (John 5:28-29). He promised that everyone would be raised to eternal existence.

How many kinds of resurrection are there? Although all will come forth from the graves, they will not all be in the same place throughout eternity. There are two types of resurrection. One resurrection is for those who have done good (John 5:29), that is, having done good as God sees good. It is accepting His provision from sin, accepting Christ as one's personal Savior. Only those who know and trust Christ will be raised from the dead in the first kind of resurrection (cf. Revelation 20:6).

The second type of resurrection is for those who have done evil. That is the resurrection of damnation or judgment (John 5:29). Who are those who have done evil? They are the ones who have not received Christ as Savior, those who have not done good as God sees it. They will also be raised, but they will not be in the same place as believers.

Although the unsaved will have eternal existence, they will not be eternally with the Lord.

They will be separated from Him and cast into the lake of fire. That is the second death (Revelation 20:14).

When will those resurrections take place? The first resurrection, for those who have done good, occurs in several different stages, or phases, rather than all at once. For example, Christ is the first fruits, and then later those who are Christ's at His coming will be raised (1 Corinthians 15:23). Although there is a lot of time between the resurrection of Christ and those who are His, both groups are part of the first kind of resurrection. The kind is the same, but the time of their resurrection is different.

When will the stages, or phases, of the first resurrection occur? The first one is Christ, the firstfruits. He is the first one to be raised, never to die again (1 Corinthians 15:23). Although others, like Jairus's daughter, the woman of Nain's son, and Lazarus all were raised, Jesus Christ was raised never to die again. That will also be true when we are raised. We will be changed and have bodies like the glorious body of Christ (1 Corinthians 15:51). We will never die again.

After Christ, the next group to be raised is the church. That group, also part of the first resurrection, will be raised at the rapture when Christ will come for the church, to receive unto Him both those who are dead and alive (1 Thessalonians 4:16–17).

A third group that will be raised as part of the

first resurrection is the Tribulation saints. That group consists of those who have died during the coming Tribulation period and know Christ as Savior. Many of those will be martyred for their testimony. They will be raised at the second coming of Christ, the time immediately after the Tribulation when Christ returns to set up His kingdom here on the earth (Revelation 20:4).

Another group that will be part of this resurrection is the Old Testament saints, those saved during Old Testament times. Those people will be raised when Christ comes to set up His kingdom on the earth, the same time as Tribulation saints are raised (Daniel 12:1-2).

What happens in the second resurrection, the resurrection of the wicked? All of those people will be raised at one time. They will be raised to stand before the great white throne judgment, and then be cast into the lake of fire (Revelation 20:11-15).

That judgment will occur right after the Millennium, the thousand-year reign of Christ upon the earth. Somewhere between heaven and earth will appear a great white throne. White is the symbol of God's holiness, purity, and sinless character. Christ Himself will be the judge, and the unrighteous will stand before Him.

Those raised at that time will be all those who are not found written in the Lamb's book of life. God will raise them from the dead, and they will stand before Him.

What will happen at that judgment? Two sets of books will be opened and examined. The first set is the Lamb's book of life (Revelation 20:12), the list of all who have trusted Christ as Savior. The names of none of those standing before the Lord at this time will be found in this book.

The other set of books is a book of works. Those are books that contain the works done by the unsaved. Their works indicate their faith, for "faith without works is dead" (James 2:26). This is then a double check as to who should be at this judgment. These people's wicked works will indicate their lack of faith and their sinful condition.

Their works will also show the grace of God. Although God always deals with man by grace, man deals with himself by works. That is why man tries to work his way to heaven. In this judgment, however, God will use man's own standard, that of works, to show he is completely lost. His righteousnesses are as filthy rags (Isaiah 64:6). No one will be able to measure up to the righteousness God requires to enter God's heaven.

What are the results of the great white throne judgment? First, there will be eternal death. That does not mean man will cease to be, but rather that there will be eternal separation from God. In addition, the unsaved will be cast into the lake of fire, the place of everlasting torment for the wicked (Matthew 25:41, 46). The unsaved will be everlastingly punished for their sin.

By way of complete contrast, those who have trusted Christ as their Savior during this age will stand before the Lord at the judgment seat of Christ. What is this judgment? It is not a court of condemnation, as with the great white throne judgment, but rather is a time of commendation. The original word that is used of this judgment (*bema,* 2 Corinthians 5:10), means a judging stand, or place of commendation. For instance, when footraces were run near the city of Corinth, the winner would come and stand before this judging stand and receive his victor's crown. In the same way, God says that all believers in this age must stand before the judging stand of Christ and there be rewarded for our works.

What is the basis of this judgment? First, there must be a proper foundation (1 Corinthians 3:11). That foundation can only be Jesus Christ. That is why this judgment is only for believers.

The other basis is the kind of materials we have used to build our lives for Him. Six materials are possible; gold, silver, precious stones, wood, hay, or stubble (1 Corinthians 3:12). Although six materials are mentioned, however, there are in reality only two types. There is that which is permanent, that which God puts into the life: gold, silver, precious stones. And there is that which is perishable, that which we try to put into our own lives: wood, hay, and stubble. The basis of this judgment is whether or not God was allowed to work through us, or whether we were trying to do things in our own self-effort. It has to do with our attitude and motivation in working for Jesus Christ today. To work for Him, there must be not only activity but also a right attitude—an attitude that puts Him first. It is because of a right attitude that those believers will be rewarded when they stand before Him.

What will happen when they are rewarded? God promises that the crowns they receive will be cast in an act of worship at His feet (Revelation 4:4, 11). The great embarrassment is going to come when there will be those with little or nothing to offer to Him.

When will that judgment take place? It may occur right after the church is raptured, at the time Christ comes for it. It is then that believers will stand before Him and be rewarded by Him.

Is there life after death? Although a lot of people today may not be sure, the Scriptures answer a resounding, "Yes!" There is life after death for both believers and unbelievers. But how much better to know Christ today as one's own Savior, than to stand before Him in a future day as judge! Is it not better to be at the judgment seat of Christ than to be at the great white throne judgment?

13
Where Will We
Spend Eternity?

"I would like more space in the breakfast area," said Mary, "and the family room needs to be larger, too."

She and her husband, Bob, were meeting with the architect over the design of their new home. This was the third house they had built, and Mary and Bob already had talked about it for over two years.

"We've made a lot of mistakes on our previous houses," she told Bob, "but I guess that's the way we learn. In this house, though, I would like all my dreams to come true."

"Do you really think that's possible?" questioned Bob, who had heard Mary say the same thing about the others. "I'm not sure there is a *perfect* house. All seem to lack something. But, Mary, if we could build a real dream house, what would it have?"

"We have to have enough space, and certainly enough different rooms," Mary countered. "And, you know, I have to have enough closet space. There's never enough room for everything. And a desk in the kitchen—I do need that. The laundry room has to be convenient. And I also need...."

The list went on and on, and Bob made his list, too. Now they were talking to the architect and would have to compromise on many things. Finally, they would settle for the essential things in light of what they could afford. But if they could have their own dream house, what would it be like?

All of us have thought about what we would consider to be the perfect home. And although there are some beautiful places on this earth, those who have lived there awhile have always found something wrong with them. But one day God is going to make for all believers a beautiful place, a place that will be a perfect home for all of us.

One day the heaven and earth we know will be destroyed (2 Peter 3:7, 10–13). The very makeup of this world will pass away, for it has been affected by sin. It is then that God will create a new heaven and a new earth (Revelation 21:1). There will be a new kind of heaven and a new kind of earth, although the geographical boundaries may be very similar to what we know today. This will be a perfect heaven and earth, a place without sin.

In addition, the Lord will create a holy city, the new Jerusalem (Revelation 21:2). The name of this city is interesting. It is called "holy" because it will have in it only those who are holy, who have been perfect in God's sight. It is called "new" since it is in contrast to the present city of Jerusalem. The present city, whose name means "city of peace," has been the site of many wars throughout history. It has been destroyed several times. Even now it is the center of contention and is yet to endure much bloodshed.

The new Jerusalem will be different. It will be perfect since it will be created by God. It will not be built from the earth nor from the materials of this earth. The preparation of it is "as a bride adorned for her husband" (Revelation 21:2). Just as a bride is perfectly prepared for her husband on her wedding day, so this city will have been perfectly prepared by God as it comes from Him out of heaven. This will be the permanent dwelling place of the saints of God throughout all eternity.

Who is the builder of that city? It is none other than God Himself. He is the one who has built it, and therefore it will be perfect as He is perfect

(Hebrews 11:10). That was what Abraham looked for. Although many believe Abraham was looking for a land or a country, he was actually looking for a city. That will be what God gives all of us who know Him as our eternal abiding place.

Jesus promised He was going to prepare that place (John 14:2). He is furnishing it, decorating it beautifully. That He has been gone such a long time must mean it will be an exquisite place.

Of what will the city be built? It is described in terms of materials we know today, although it will be built by God. The materials are gold, pearls, and precious stones (Revelation 21:18-21). Beautiful stones are mentioned as the covering of Satan before he fell from heaven (Ezekiel 28:13). They are also used to describe the place of Israel in the millennial kingdom (Isaiah 54:11-12). As such, they may picture that the believer will in the future have as much or more than Satan had before he fell. Could it be that the building of our lives on the permanent materials of the future (cf. 1 Corinthians 3:12) should remind us of our future abiding place?

Around the city will be a great wall, a wall of protection and beautiful decoration (Revelation 21:17-18). It will be made of jasper, a stone that is a pure crystal. Perhaps that will emphasize the holiness of the city since it symbolizes God's deity.

The city will have twelve foundations (Revelation 21:14). It is in the foundations that the names of the twelve apostles are found. As the church is built upon the foundation of the apostles (Ephesians 2:20), so they will be memorialized in the foundations of the New Jerusalem.

The city will have twelve gates (Revelation 21:12-13). Since the city is constructed four-square, there will be three gates on each side of the city. The gates will have in them the names of the twelve tribes of Israel. Although God deals with Israel in many different ways, here in the heavenly city will be those who have been saved and who are of Israel.

Each gate is formed of one single pearl (Revelation 21:21), symbolizing beauty, purity, and unity. At each gate will be an angel to watch over those entering the city and to keep out anything that would defile the city (Revelation 21:12,27). Angels who serve the Lord will continue to serve Him throughout eternity. The gates are never closed, so there will always be free access to the presence of God (Revelation 21:25).

What will the streets be like in this city from heaven? They will be of pure gold (Revelation 21:21). The original word translated "street" literally means "open place." It is the custom of modern cities to have malls and many open places between buildings. So it will be in the heavenly city. There is no description of any grass, but rather all the open places, the space between buildings, will be of pure gold.

What does pure gold look like? When gold is refined, it is impossible today to make it completely pure. In fact, it is the impurity in gold that gives it its color. But if gold could be completely refined in an absolutely pure form, it well may be transparent. This is the way the Spirit of God describes the gold of this city (Revelation 21:21).

What is the illumination of the city? That which enlightens the whole city is the glory of God and the Lamb. The city has no need of any sun, stars, or other illuminating body. Rather, the glory of the Lord Himself will provide the light for the city (Revelation 21:23; 22:5).

What is the size of the city? It is 12,000 furlongs, or 1500 miles, in each direction (Revelation 21:16). Since the city is foursquare, the base of it would be 1500 miles in each direction, and it would be 1500 miles high. This is a huge amount of space. It is the distance halfway across the United States. But since this city will hold the redeemed of all ages, it naturally would have to be large.

The shape of the city may be in the form of a cube, for that geometric figure answers the description of its length, breadth, and height being equal (Revelation 21:16). But a pyramid also answers that same description. If it were a pyramid, that would help us understand how the river of God could encircle it from the top to the bottom (Revelation 22:1). Evidently it will start at a very narrow base at the top, and then wind around throughout the city as it goes to the bottom.

Who are the people that will inhabit the new Jerusalem? Certainly they must all be believers, for nothing can enter the city that would defile it (Revelation 21:27). Moreover, unbelievers will be throughout eternity in the lake of fire (Revelation 20:15).

But God carefully describes who it will be who will dwell in this heavenly city. First, there is an innumerable company of angels (Hebrews 12:22–24). Those would be good angels, those who have not sinned against God. Some of them will stand at the gates of the city. Others may be worshiping God continually (cf. Isaiah 6; Revelation 4).

In addition to angels there also will be the church. This is that group of people who know Christ as Savior in this age. They are the ones who have been called out from this world, both Jew and Gentile, and are united to the Body of Christ. One day they will be caught up to be with Christ, rewarded by Him, and will return with Him when He sets up His kingdom upon this earth. Their eternal abode will be the new Jerusalem.

God Himself will also be in this city, and His glory will fill the place. In addition, the spirits of just men made perfect, or Old Testament saints, will inhabit the city. This will be the place where Abraham and all the other Old Testament believers will be.

Jesus Himself, the mediator of the new covenant, will be present in the city. It is the glory of the Lamb that will enlighten the city, providing light for all.

When will the city come down upon the earth? Some believe it will appear only during the eternal state, the time after the reign of Christ upon the earth. That is because it is mentioned in the book of Revelation after the millennial reign of Christ.

A careful study of this passage shows there will be a tree in the city for the healing of the nations (Revelation 22:2). Nothing that would defile it will be allowed to enter (Revelation 21:27).

Perhaps a better view is that this passage is describing the city from heaven, not when it will appear. Because it is an eternal city from heaven and because it will have evidences of the Millennium, perhaps it appears in both the Millennium and the eternal state. During the Millennium it would come down and hover over the old city of Jerusalem, since there is not enough room upon this earth to house it in that part of the world in addition to the old city which is necessary during that time. At the end of the Millennium, it would be taken up to heaven while this present heaven and earth are destroyed and a new one is created. Finally, it would come down upon the new earth after it has been created by God.

If that were to take place, it would help us

understand the Millennium better. During that time there will be on the earth people with natural bodies, who will bear children. At the same time there will also be those with glorified bodies. The ones who would have glorified bodies at that time, the church, Old Testament saints, Tribulation saints, would be dwelling in the new Jerusalem, even though they would have access to the earth. Angels would need to guard the gates of the city so nothing during that time could enter that would defile the city. During the eternal state, when the city is upon the new earth, that would not be necessary.

God has a wonderful destiny for all who know Him. The place He has promised us is a place of beauty, exquisiteness, and elaborate decoration. It is a place yet to come upon the earth. But heaven is not only a place, it is also a person. It is having fellowship with God forever. It is being where He is.

You and I can now enjoy that heavenly life by enjoying His fellowship. We can be demonstrating the life of Christ to a world that needs to know Him. One day He will be coming for us and taking us to be with Him. One day we will be in our eternal abiding place especially made for us by Him. Should we not be living for Him now as we look for His return?